BLEEDING NIPPLES

What it takes to be a successful runner

Publishing Information

Published 2010 by Bleeding Nipples
bleedingauthor@gmail.com

Printed and bound by Lulu.com

Cover image © Rich Kenington www.theracephotographer.com

The publisher and author have done their best to ensure the accuracy and currency of all information in *Bleeding Nipples*; however, they can accept no responsibility for any loss or inconvenience sustained by any reader as a result of its information or advice. Neither the author nor the publisher may be held responsible for any action, claim, loss or injury howsoever resulting from the use of this book or any information contained in it. Readers must obtain their own professional medical advice before relying on or otherwise making use of any medical information contained in this book.

© Rocco Giordano, 2010
All rights reserved
ISBN: 978-1-4466-7162-7

BLEEDING NIPPLES

What it takes to be a successful runner

by
Rocco Giordano

ACKNOWLEDGMENTS

My thanks go to all, from my parents onwards, who have helped me become a half decent runner, even if it is a mixed blessing! Thank you also to Kate Berens whose attention to detail in editing this book far exceeded my own.

WARM UP

Take everything in this book with a pinch of salt! That's my first piece of advice. Not too big a pinch, however, as too much salt is bad for you. Look at all those unhealthy Italians trailing around, crippled by the years of consuming over-salted pasta, risotto dishes and olives. Or maybe a lot of salt *is* good for us runners because it wards off those end-of-marathon, killer cramps and replaces all the minerals we sweat out into our sodden T-shirts.

Let's compromise and just stick to a small pinch of the stuff, literally and metaphorically, as compromise definitely is healthy. In running, if you don't compromise, if you don't take your pinch of salt, you become obsessed. An obsession with running takes over your life, you think about it all the time and you can end up losing your job and ruining your relationship as a direct result. In fact, taking up serious running should be top of the list of the 'fifty ways to leave your lover'. You leave them to go out running once too often and they leave *you* for good. Perhaps you have already reached the stage of addiction or dependency in which all that sounds worth it or desirable, in which case you may need medical help.

Assuming that you are not just running your way out of a marriage and that you quite like having a bit of cash in your pocket, we can move on. After all, if you are reading this, the chances are that you are not drowning in sponsorship money and the amount of gold that you could get from melting down a lifetime's supply of finishers' medals won't even buy you a post-race massage, let alone your petrol to get home.

This book is about how to improve your running. Even if you know most of what is in here already, a hefty jog (sorry, we don't jog, we *run*) to the memory is always useful. Not only that, it might give you a new perspective on this God-given endorphin trip that forces us out of our front door and brings us home, possibly feeling knackered, even in pain, but always that little bit happier, that little bit more smug, than we would have been if we had not bothered to get our backsides off the sofa in the first place.

I will not be treading carefully as, at threshold pace, we stride across the entire landscape of running hang-ups and taboos. The gamut of running magazines and coaching websites is strewn with euphemisms and political correctness. I call a spade a spade, a roll of fat a roll of fat, and a hard effort is not a hard effort unless your face is contorted in pain at the end of it. There can be gain without pain, but no progress without honesty, and the truth can hurt.

This book is for you, whether you are about to buy your first pair of running shoes or whether the soles on your **racing flats** are worn from one too many sub-1;15 half-marathons. Maybe you still think a racing flat is that apartment you can't afford, overlooking the Monaco Grand Prix circuit (in which case check out the glossary!) or possibly you've run the Nice to Cannes marathon and took in that same circuit as a training run. It makes no odds. We all need advice and we all need a smile put on our faces.

We will be delving into the intricacies of different types of training and all the other factors that can influence your performance, from work to holidays, sleep to over-arousal (sexual and anticipatory), self-doubt to over-confidence. Littered throughout these pages will be tips to help you get to the finish line quicker, many of which you can apply from tomorrow with no extra effort. So make yourself an extra cup of tea or coffee (yes, they improve performance too), concentrate and enjoy!

MILE 1

CHOOSE YOUR PARENTS

When I start reading a book I do not give the author the benefit of the doubt, and I run out of patience *very* quickly. By the end of the first paragraph of a Harry Potter novel my head is lolling backwards, my eyelids are getting heavy, my lower jaw is extending towards the floor and you can count the seconds to my first snore. That's another side-effect of heavy training and you will soon find, as you build up the miles, that dozing off for a ten-minute power-nap is never a problem. Trouble is, it sometimes happens during a meeting or even, in my case, whilst teaching French to a class full of pupils. A hail of paper aeroplanes soon woke me up from that particular little snooze! If you are like me and the shutters are already starting to come down over your pupils (the eye sort, not the student sort), just pinch yourself hard and stay awake for the next few sentences. I am about to summarise the whole book in five short instructions...

Run more! Run faster! Shed some fat! Recover properly! Race intelligently!

That's it! Do all of those things and I guarantee that you will improve your times. Now, sink into your armchair and dream away. Or, better still, lace up your trainers and push off out of that door for a session of **hill reps** (see glossary).

Right, now that we have that impetuous lot out of the way (they will be back later, with plenty of time and energy to read as they nurse their sore **Achilles** tendons), I can let the rest of you know the *whole* truth. It is indeed as simple as those five commands suggest, but actually carrying them out requires a complex amalgamation of willpower, training and knowledge of how to maximise your potential. How to put these things together and actually reach a point where you are covering the ground faster than before, that is what this book is aiming to make you understand.

I'm not one of these 'the older I get the faster I was' types and I certainly don't want to bore you with my **palmarès**, as they call them in the world of cycling. Suffice to say that my attic contains a few pillow cases which in turn are struggling to contain the ever-increasing collection of cheaply produced winners' trophies that come my way at events like 'The Middle Of Nowhere 10k' or the 'Hard To Find On The Internet Half-Marathon' or even the 'Twisty Turny Triple-Sprint Triathlon'. To be fair to myself, I did do quite well in the small and exclusive world of **duathlon** and even represented Great Britain at elite level once, though on the basis of my performance, 'Great' was a bit of a misnomer. Anyway, what I was getting round to saying was that when I was a budding triathlete, full of enthusiasm and searching for every training tip possible to get me to the top, I went to a 'training day' run by the coach to a British World Champion. The first words of his opening seminar were along these lines: 'Over 85 percent of athletic ability is down to genetics, and as you can't choose your parents there is nothing you can do about it!'

Well, you can imagine how inspired I was by that opening gambit! I looked around the room. Some older athletes were smiling wryly but most of the Lycra-clad audience, like me, seemed ready to go home and give salsa dancing a crack instead.

Now what Mr Motivator said might be true in that our chances of ever becoming undisputed world champions are very much determined by genetics, but our ability to dramatically, nay *drastically* improve our current levels of performance are almost entirely *un*constrained by our DNA. Of course age must take its toll, but I am yet to meet anyone of any age who can convince me that there is no way I can get them to run significantly faster.

Take Cravatta for example. No word of a lie, this guy runs in a shirt and tie all year round. That's how he got his name ('cravatta' means 'tie' in Italian). His top button, without fail, is firmly secured, and his deer-stalker hat never leaves his head. He always seems to be outdoors, lugging his orange Sainsbury's bags home, gazing at the river, or, as is usually the case, just running. If you don't *see* him coming, you will undoubtedly hear him. He's one of those runners that sound like a cross between a steam train and a wheezing wild boar. That doesn't slow him down though! At 65 years of age he runs marathons in three hours and twenty minutes. Imagine what he could do in a running vest! Not only that, his training predominantly consists of three-hour runs, week after week, season after season. Now I do believe in 'getting the miles in' and there is a lot of truth in the maxim that 'miles make champions', but if old Cravatta just eased back a bit in the lead-up to the London Marathon and introduced a bit of **speedwork** (much more on this later), then he could be running times that would put competitive runners to shame who are twenty years his junior. Things are moving in the right direction, I have to report, as he has recently been spotted wearing shorts and trainers as opposed to his suit-trousers and white plimsolls.

Of course most cases are not as clear cut as Cravatta's but the message here is that *you* can get quicker. Not just a little bit quicker, so that you can finish in front of your perennial rival or your drinking buddies, but enough to leave them gazing into their empty pint glasses, wondering if your performance was part of a beer-induced mirage. There is a proviso however! Don't let *them* read this book too!

Whatever body shape you have, you have the potential to be a good runner. We are born with a need to run, to escape or to follow. Certainly if you look more like Linford Christie than

Haile Gebrselassie, then a two-hour marathon is unlikely, but you would be surprised at the shapes and sizes that make their way onto the podium at distance races. Often the lanky, tanned, sunglasses-wearing poseurs who look the part are put to shame by the round-shouldered, pale-faced weekend warriors who know what they are doing and are not afraid of a bit of hard work!

If you already consider yourself a fast runner and you train intelligently all year round it will evidently be that much harder for you to make, figuratively speaking, huge steps forward. Nevertheless, later chapters will provide you with a checklist of essential elements which will then be moulded into the constituent parts of a plan that will bring your running on, figuratively and perhaps literally, in leaps and bounds! I speak from personal experience when I say that even those of us who have been running competitively for nigh on twenty years can look forward to rewriting our personal record books if we get it all right. On the other hand, the newer you are to running, the easier it is to knock chunks off your times with startling regularity. Ahh those are great days indeed... as you check your watch while sprinting for the line and can hardly believe your eyes as three minutes have disappeared from what you saw there a month before as you crossed the finish of your previous **10k**. In fact, it is not uncommon for runners who have only recently lost their racing virginity to start calculating how long it will take them, given their current rate of improvement, to start breaking world records.

Consider Esmerelda (I won't use her real name because if I did she might pay someone to break my kneecaps, which in turn would make running rather problematic). She was, let's say, a little overweight. No, I promised in the introduction that there would only be straight-talking in this book. She was fat. She decided to take up running a few months ago to do something about it. The pounds fell off her and she became confident enough to start entering a weekly five-kilometre race. So far her times have progressed from 33 minutes to 30, 28, 27, 26, and now down to 24. She told me last week that, even allowing for a fifty percent slowing of the rate of progression, she will be challenging Tirunesh Dibaba's world record of 14 minutes and 11 seconds within five months. As for the London 2012 Olympics, well she reckons that she should just manage to lap the second-placed athlete before the finish line.

She knows and we all know that she is living in a dreamland, but this optimism and the ease with which we can better our performances when we embark on our running careers, act as fantastic motivators. Fat or thin, old or young, fit as a fiddle or fit to drop, half the battle is finding the right motivation. One thing is for sure and that is that you will never maximise your potential, never achieve those times that at the moment seem so far out of reach, unless you really, really…

MILE 2

WANT IT!

If it doesn't really matter to you, you won't make it happen. Just as footballers won't win titles for their teams if they care more about their obscenely huge pay packets than the victory, results don't come for you by thinking 'wouldn't it be nice to win the London Marathon one day' or 'this year I'll train a little bit harder'

Watch those Africans as they go through the tape on The Mall, twenty-six point two miles of pain burning in their legs and etched on their faces. As often as not they actually puke up from the effort. Watch those Tour de France riders, twenty-odd days of two-hundred-kilometre stages behind them, racing up the final climb of the day, draining the last molecule of glucose from their body to cross the line in a final sprint and then collapsing tearfully into the arms of their **Directeur Sportif** They wanted it, not just on the day of the race, but for the 365 days of every year since they started serious competition. I'm sorry, but if you want to excel in your own personal endeavour, your own 'Tour de Yourself', you have to want it *bad*. It's not the sort of expression I would normally use, but it carries in it a suggestion of the attitude and aggression needed by all except the most naturally gifted in order to go beyond the level that others would expect to see us at. Maybe you are thinking to yourself, 'Blimey this is a bit heavy! I only want to run a bit quicker'. Run a *bit* quicker you will, for that is what you want, but if you want to run a *lot* quicker, I repeat, you have to want it *bad*. I remember watching the Bath Triathlon on TV in the early nineties: Spencer Smith, the British World Champion, was pulling away from Simon Lessing, his major rival, in the bike section of the race. His father was encouraging him from the side of the road. His choice of words? 'Give it to 'em bad!' In four and a half words he was actually saying something much more complex, on the lines of 'you have worked for this, now make it count! Don't be afraid to go beyond your perceived limits and don't show any mercy to your opposition!'

By following the more technical advice in this book and elsewhere you can still aim to smash your previous bests, but without that desire you will never be as good as you could have been. To get to your 'max' you must not be obsessed with your running but, like a pet dog, you have to think about it and look after it every day. Your running must not become the be all and end all of your existence. If it does, the chances are that you will end up ruining your family life, injuring yourself and becoming miserable, all of which will in any case actually bring your performance levels down, not up.

Your running *does* have to matter to you more than staying behind an extra hour at work just to please your boss. It must matter more than the pleasure you might get from a second slice of warm chocolate fudge-cake, even if you have already decided to give the cream a miss. It needs to matter more than your weekend lie-in, Saturday and Sunday! Finally, even if Ryanair are going to charge you an extra forty quid for the bag, your running must be important enough to make you take your running shorts, socks, trainers and umpteen T-shirts with you on holiday. Your pre-departure holiday checklist should read 'Trainers, Passport, Money' – in that order!

For every week you 'want it bad' you will put in a productive week's training, no doubt about it, and if you keep the desire going long enough you will get to the morning of your target race with a quiet confidence. You will toe the start line knowing you can cope with the demands of the event, and with your mind free to actually focus on *how* best to run a great race rather than wondering *whether* you will have a great run or not.

I am sure that many of you reading this are starting to feel uneasy. 'I thought this book was going to make me smile my way to victory, not bark at me like a sergeant major on a parade ground getting his privates into line' (the sort that wear uniform that is). Well, '*At Ease!*', because if you are simply not a 'want it bad' sort of person, if you are far too nice, far too soft and cuddly on the inside for all that, there are a few nifty little ways of making your performance matter to you as much as it does to those angry balls of testosterone that even shout 'I want it bad!' in their sleep.

One key way is to involve other people. A big training chart on a kitchen cupboard might be enough. Surely you don't want your family or housemates laughing at you after every session you fail to tick off as successfully completed? The fear of humiliation will spur you on. Maybe you need to tell your friends and workmates how quick you are going to be. Once you have set your goal (more on that later), declare it as your aim to people you know well. Again, you will not want to lose face and no inclement weather or feeling of tiredness will prevent you from sticking to your plan and achieving your target.

Perhaps you can involve some fund-raising or charity donation in your self motivation technique. So often we hear those weary finishers repeating to the marathon or Great North Run television cameras, 'I had to finish it for the sake of Tiddywinkles, the injured hedgehog charity that is so close to my heart.' (Other worthy causes do exist.)

Don't care what others think? Don't want to run for a (that's just for **fun runners**') charity? Try imposing a strict punishment and reward system on yourself: If you miss a session you don't eat dinner that day. Simple as that. If you run lazy you run an extra half hour the next day. Too feeble, too lily-livered even for that? One final option remains! Get together as much money as you would spend on a holiday and give it to someone you trust. Make them sign a legally binding document to say that they will not give it back to you unless you achieve your next major aim in your running. Effectively you are putting a whacking great bet on yourself, or, looking at it another way, you are instantly turning yourself into a professional athlete! Now you will want it *bad*, believe me, *very bad*!

Be quietly pleased with yourself, but never satisfied, as you clock up the successful days of training. Build on the progress you know you are making. Let wanting it gradually turn into knowing you can have it, and knowing you can have it into actually getting it. Only then take the money and take that holiday! You deserve it!

By now you must be getting fed up with the repetition of the idea that to do well enough for it to be an achievement worth writing home about, or, better still, worthy of the local newspaper, you have to make your goal as vital to you as your most basic human needs. 'But what does that mean for me as an individual?' you ask. 'I've never been there, it's not on a map, so how do I know where to head for?' Of course many of you will already have a precise idea of the races or times you are aiming for, but setting objectives, targets, goals, call them what you will, is a problem for the majority of runners. As we are about to show, it certainly needn't be!

MILE 3

BE A SMART ARSE!

How do coaches get their money and the respect of their athletes? By working with them to achieve the goals that they have set together, and, if it all goes wrong, by persuading the athletes that the failure was entirely down to them or to some other circumstance outside of the coach's control. Not surprising then that most coaches or trainers will get you to set fairly modest targets. Not surprising either that running websites and magazines will publish dozens of pages, time after time, devoted to goal-setting techniques. Ninety-nine percent of the time they are just a reworking of the SMART acronym: Targets, they tell us, should be:

- Specific
- Measurable
- Attainable
- Realistic and
- Tangible (or, in some versions, 'time-bound')

Yawn, yawn, yawn! Imagine going for an interview and being asked about what you can bring to your new workplace or company? 'Tell us about where you are aiming for, about your ambitions!' Out comes your SMART reply: 'Well, I like to be very specific and clear about what I am working towards. I will only attempt things that seem realistic and that I know I can attain. I need to be able to measure how I am getting on and everything I do has to have a clear time-limit and be definitely within my reach.' By implication, therefore, you might as well carry on: 'I won't be over-ambitious and I won't take risks.' How very inspirational! Sorry mate, but you are the weakest link! Goodbye!

I would like to propose an equally memorable acronym that puts goal-setting on another level. Instead of SMART it's ARSE and it's by far the more likely to get that part of your anatomy in gear. Targets should be:

- Autonomous
- Radical
- Stimulating and
- Enduring

See? Much more fun! Don't waste your time arsing about with a SMART approach to planning. It just means hours of working out step-by-step progressions, **macrocycles** and **mesocycles**, interim targets and session structures, which are bound to have to be revised anyway. Why? Because life is unpredictable and each one of us responds differently to the same type of training. We can all have good days and bad days, we can all get ill, we can all fall in love, and, more importantly, we can all surprise ourselves with a sudden jump in form that can blow a training plan to bits. Adopting a SMART-type approach to your running aims is a bit like the girl who says she is going to get married at the age of 26, have three kids by the time she is 32, then move to the country on her 40th birthday. Even if she spends every waking hour working towards those things and even if, as coaches will always tell you, targets can be adapted and revised, much of it is still bound to be out of her control. On top of that, even if the aims are achieved, I would suggest that the very fact they were chosen within rigid limits and in the sure knowledge that they were attainable, makes them less worthwhile.

This brings us to the ARSE of the matter. A is for Autonomous, because all your goals have to depend on you and you alone. You cannot predict the state of your health on a particular race day, so don't aim for just one race. You don't know how well your rivals are going to do (especially if they read this too), so don't make beating a particular person your target either. Chances are that will happen anyway, but treat it as an added bonus. An example of an autonomous aim might be 'to get up at six o'clock, six days a week, and run for at least half an hour if I am physically capable of it'.

Now we must add the R for Radical. Autonomous, radical, we are beginning to sound like a revolutionary political movement, and why not? Revolutions can create real and lasting change. SMART targets are more like a politically correct centre-left coalition: all process and no substance. A goal needs to be radical because we don't want to be left wondering what might have been. A realistic, attainable goal might leave us satisfied upon completion, but it will not take us to the limit of our capabilities. At least, as someone once said, if we aim for the stars we might bang our heads on the ceiling. This is preferable by far to going on a course on how to climb a ladder then coming back to find somebody has already installed a lift! A radical goal might be to run at race pace for ten minutes for every biscuit or cake you eat, and to add ten minutes on to your longest run of the week for every pint of beer or glass of wine consumed in the previous seven days.

Goals also need to be exciting, to be S for Stimulating. They have to get you off your arse and out of the door. 'If I don't run now I might be five seconds slower at the next back of beyond 10k' doesn't cut it for most of us. Aim high! Aim to run all the way up a mountain! Aim to run a shorter or longer race than ever before! Aim to be able to jump up and down naked in front of a mirror and see nothing wobble except those bits that are supposed to! Aim to run faster than your mates believe you are capable of!

Don't put yourself in a position where your goal has an expiry date. This can be psychologically damaging if you don't make it and it can leave you feeling empty and directionless if you do. Don't make your goals time-bound, make them E for Enduring. In this respect we could all aim for the same thing. 'I will be as fit and fast as I possibly can be!' If you head in that direction, and later chapters will suggest how, the personal bests and race goals that might have made up your SMART targets will just come your way as a pleasant by-product. Of course you might wish to *peak* at certain times of year or even for a particular occasion, but remember there are things outside of your control that can bring disaster if you put all your eggs in one basket. A classic example of when thousands of SMART targets went to rack and ruin but the ARSEs amongst us stayed focussed and happy, was in 2001 when the Foot and Mouth Disease outbreak led to much restriction of movement and the cancellation of hundreds of running races, triathlons and other sporting events. Make your goals Enduring ones and even a national crisis won't hold you back.

ARSE is best (not in a sexual sense you understand) and those in the know have been aware of this all along. That is why a slogan like 'Race for Life' or 'Just Do It' is ten times more powerful and motivating than 'Improve your PB by two minutes with this new eighteen-week plan'.

At *my* interview, full of ARSE terminology, I will speak of inspiration, radical imagination, aiming for the top and going on for as long as is humanly possible. Bring it on Alan Sugar, bring it on!

With this strategy in mind then, how can we apply it to day to day training? How can we motivate ourselves to stride out for that extra mile in the wind, the rain and the freezing cold with which our sceptred isle is so frequently blessed? What can we write on the fridge or say to our mates in order to keep the desire burning, to keep wanting it *bad?*

The key is to know what works best for you. Start thinking, honestly and brutally, about the things that are most likely to stop you getting out there and doing the necessary. Now buy a big block of Post-its, pick up a marker pen and write, as bold and big as will fit on the note, the comment that will stop you in your tracks if you are about to grab that extra slice of cake (that one's for the cupboard door), or the slogan that will make you jump out of bed and out onto the street (that one's for the alarm clock). 'THE HOUSE IS ON FIRE' works quite well for that one, but the joke wears thin very quickly and a more incisive alternative that relates to your psyche does need to be found.

Maybe you react well to reward systems. Try 'you only get an extra pint on Friday if you run 5 miles every day till then'. (Not to be started on a Thursday, that one.) How about, 'a massage and a hot chocolate at the weekend if you stay off the crisps'? Or 'two weeks on the beach in Spain if you average over forty miles a week till the marathon.'

Another approach is to target the areas you are most sensitive about. Stick one on the bathroom mirror. 'This will not improve unless you run more!' Think about the people you would most like to impress and stick a note on your cornflakes packet or your desk at work. 'Get out there or they will laugh at you!' 'Prove to them that you can do it!' 'If Big Bob does it, so can you!'

Little rhyming couplets also work wonders for many people. As a cyclist, my favourite was 'are you riding or hiding?' This can be adapted to 'are you running or shunning?', 'training or feigning?', 'trying or shying?' Or, for the vulgar end of the market, 'Are you getting fit… or staying shit?'

Combine it with the reward idea and get 'No run, no bun!' Perhaps it is only the threat of punishment that will make you change your ways. 'Eat these biscuits', says the note on the tin, 'and you run two and a half hours tomorrow!'

Of course we haven't looked at the specifics of what your ARSE targets should be and what training methods are required to achieve them. That will depend on each individual and we will deal with training plans in later chapters. Common to all of us, however, is the need to get out there and run and, for most of us, to shed some excess pounds at the same time. Another barrier to many people, before they dare take those first nervous strides towards eventual running greatness, is not knowing what to wear. Put that on a Post-it too! 'No 200 miles this month, no new trainers!'

MILE 4

SILLY SOCKS

You can usually spot a competitive runner coming towards you, not by their speed or grace of movement (both of these are ultra-variable), but by the kit they are wearing. Mr or Ms Athlete will either be sporting a running vest which is seemingly far too lightweight for the time of year, or a race T-shirt. These often tend towards the tatty or the greying because runners feel better about themselves and run taller and prouder when displaying the name of a race they did particularly well in. Underneath they are all yearning for you to ask them, 'how did you get on in that race, then?' so that they can narrate that same story of how they achieved their latest **PB** that they have already inflicted on their running-club mates at every opportunity, boring them to tears in the process.

On a rainy day the waterproof running tops come out and are distinguishable by their excess of reflective strips. Luckily there has been a move away from the high-visibility yellow that was de rigueur for runners' hats, gloves, socks and most things in between in the early nineties. Be safe and be seen, but not at the expense of being laughed out of town or repeatedly asked when you were going to fix the pot-holes or read the meter.

The real give away, however, is in the shorts. A 'real' runner's shorts are unnecessarily brief, usually with a little slit up the side for good measure. The effect on women is to rob them of any femininity that years of pavement-pounding has not hammered out already. These minimal pieces of flapping polyester, masquerading as technical running apparel, do no favours for the male of the species either. Indeed they provide, all too clearly, convincing evidence that running causes marked genital shrinkage. The theory goes that as we run our blood supply is concentrated in the working muscles and vital organs, which is why fingers and toes and other extremities also tend to be the first bits to get cold. The reproductive organs are obviously not considered vital while moving at speed, though it might be fun to try and prove otherwise... As for the few blokes whose testosterone levels will not succumb to the laws of biological self-preservation and who would look more at home on the start line of a hundred-metre race, even at the end of a marathon, an extra pair of shorts or some comfortable underwear is recommended to reduce the risk of arrest for indecent exposure.

A **non-runner**, which is a category slightly preferable, in most hardened endurance athletes' eyes, to that of **fun runner**, has a completely different aspect. Taking up much more of the pavement, they have a running wardrobe which can be best described as baggy, not to say loose, or even saggy. Indeed the length and width of the shorts are usually inversely proportional to the speed and ability of the runner. The top half of the outfit usually consists of a gangsta-style hoodie, a sweat-stained 'cheapie' from the likes of Sports Direct, or a logo-splattered piece of nonsense that was worn to the pub the night before.

Stop right there! Before we even get to the nitty-gritty of the silly socks and the even sillier trainers, let me make a couple of things clear amongst all these generalisations. Firstly, you cannot always judge a book by its cover, and secondly, I have a lot more time for the guy or girl going out to do their best in whatever gear they have available, than I do for the poseurs with their training-camp tans, Oakley sunglasses and all the guts of a filleted anchovy. Never let the running fashion-police get to you! One day you will turn the tables on them and it will feel great!

Just as the tyres are vital to the performance of a Formula 1 car, so the socks and shoes we choose to wear are crucial to fulfilling our potential as runners. Even though what is in your legs is clearly more important than what is on the end of them, or indeed between them, a poor choice of sock can ruin your race, especially over the longer distances. The function of the sock is to provide comfort and prevent blisters. It must, therefore, not be so short so as not to cover the parts of the foot where the shoe could rub against it. This is particularly vital at the back of the ankle, in the area of the **Achilles** tendon, where a blister can linger for weeks and cause a lot of pain. It can also mean that you will end up having to buy yourself a new pair of trainers so as to change the pressure point. Most good running socks have two layers of material, which reduces the friction against your skin and goes a long way towards guaranteeing a blister-free ride. These socks are not cheap and if they happen to all be in the wash when you are ready and set to head out for a fast ten-miler, the low budget alternative is to smear petroleum jelly on the inside of the heel of the shoe and any other potentially painful areas.

While we are on the subject of Vaseline (other petroleum jelly products are available), it really is wonderful stuff and should be right near the top of your **race-bag checklist** Once you are ready to slather it on, remember ANGST (Armpits, Nipples, Groin, Shoes and Toes). All those sensitive areas are thus protected and we avoid the pain and embarrassment of the bleeding-nipple look, which leads to blood-stained T-shirt disease and eventually to permanently-plastered-breast syndrome. Vaseline also keeps the cold out. Toes can be kept feeling toasty and in freezing conditions a dab on the nose, lips and ears can also work wonders.

Socks have gone high-tech in recent years and, largely thanks to Paula Radcliffe, we have had to witness the rise in popularity of what I call the Silly Sock. You know the ones I mean: they come up to just below the knee and seemingly stay up by magic all the way to the finish line. Thank goodness for that, otherwise we would need the suspender-belt as well, which would just add to the 'straight out of Ann Summers' appearance which they already evoke. The theory is that they help ward off cramps by keeping the lower-leg warm and permanently massaged. Anecdotal evidence suggests there may be some truth in this and I would not discourage their use. One of the few redeeming features of a decent runner's physique, however, is the finely sculpted calf muscle and to hide it from view seems a real shame, especially as it is also at the expense of looking at worst like an escapee from a politicians' 'private members' club, or at best like a semi-reformed Morris Dancer.

The idea that clothing can not only provide comfort and protect you, but also actively improve athletic performance, seems to have spread from the feet upwards. First it was rugby players, then triathletes, and now runners who are showing off their muscle definition, puny as it may be, through the figure-hugging material of the Skins products and their like. Whether they actually facilitate muscle movement or help recovery is very much open to debate. Not only that, I set an upper limit of fifty quid on a pair of trainers, so I am hardly likely to spend the same on a sleeveless T-shirt, however many lingering little looks it might attract from members of the opposite sex (or the same sex for that matter).

'Fifty quid limit for a pair of trainers!' I hear you squawk in disbelief. Well yes, in fact it's a while since I exceeded the £35 mark! No, I don't wear tennis shoes, no, I don't make them myself, and no I don't travel to Korea to nick them straight from the sweat-shop! I feel a bit guilty about this next bit of advice, as I think specialist running shops do a great job in general and I have benefitted from their support over the years through personal sponsorship, generous prizes and support for races I have organised. A good running shop will be staffed by people who know a lot about trainers and a lot about running. They might analyse your gait and even film you, but the essential thing is that they advise you properly. They will size you up, talk to you about what you actually want the shoes for (everyday training, **speedwork**, racing, off-road events, etc) and help you choose a shoe that fits *you* properly and is fit for purpose. Hopefully they will not always guide you towards the brand with which their shop has a special relationship.

This is the naughty bit! Once you have found the shoe you want, you say 'thank you very much' and walk out. Before you do so, you could buy some socks or energy gels (more on them much later) to appease your conscience. Knowing the size (preferably in UK, USA and European numbers), the approximate weight, the type and the necessary characteristics of the desired footwear, your next port of call is your computer. Scour the internet and you will find if not the exact same shoe, then the equivalent last year's model or something as near as makes no difference, for a substantially reduced price. In case they arrive and don't suit, make sure you have the option of sending them back!

Even cheaper of course is to follow in the steps of Zola Budd and Ron Hill, amongst others, and run barefoot! The latest advertising from manufacturers like Nike and Newton extols the brilliance of their new models by saying how they just mould themselves to shape of the foot itself. Barefoot is all very well if you are lightweight, have perfect style, and live in one of the few remaining areas of this green and pleasant land that has not become grey and unpleasant. Even if you can dodge the hypodermic needles, dogs' mess and fast food packaging, the chances of cutting yourself on a sharp piece of gravel or a broken bottle are pretty much odds on.

If you want technical information on which trainers to buy, look elsewhere. Just as cyclists should be more worried about riding their bikes than polishing them, so runners should be more concerned about getting the miles in than what their feet are in. Procrastination is a much bigger problem than **pronation** and too much supper will slow you down far more than any **supination**. Have a look at the soles of your running shoes that you have used for a while. If one side of the shoe is markedly more worn than the other then you may need a special shoe. Try to stay clear of **orthotics** unless absolutely necessary as they tend to cause problems in the long term, particularly if you find your style altering as a result of the body trying to compensate for the perceived change in posture. If finding a shoe that fits well and feels right is a real problem, get as much advice as you can, not just from running shops but also from an osteopath who specialises in running injuries and whatever you do, don't give up!

Remember that it takes a long while to 'run a shoe in'. For an average trainer to become supple enough to be used in a race, a good three weeks of regular running is required. Those of us light and lucky enough to be able to use very lightweight shoes (230 grams or under) may need less, but it is always a mistake to race in a new pair of shoes. Try to love your favourite pair of racers. Just putting them on should make you feel bouncy and on your toes. It should feel *wrong* to run slowly in your **racing flats**

How many pairs of trainers you have on the go depends on your mileage levels, your budget, and the types of events you take part in. When you start, a 'one shoe fits all' policy might suffice but when you begin to race you will want a lighter pair that can easily give you a ten percent advantage. The maxim here is 'train heavy, race light'! Adding weight to your feet in your regular running will strengthen them, and your ankles too. On the days when speed counts, off come the bricks, on go the feathers and you will be ready to fly.

A pair of shoes with decent cushioning and a lightweight alternative for your speedy sessions are all that is usually required. If you run off-road a lot you will also need something with good grip, particularly in the winter months. Racing multi-terrain and cross-country races presents a footwear-purchasing dilemma as many courses are best run in normal road **racing flats** while others require **spikes** and yet others are best covered in a fell-running shoe or **waffle** which has a studded sole. For racing the best-fit option has to be the **spikes**, but make sure they are fitted with short ones. You may clatter a bit on the road sections of a **multi-terrain race** but you will not slip over and you should feel light and bouncy. In **spikes** you can attack the uphill sections, the downhill stretches and the corners at race speed with confidence, and you also get a weapon to cut up your rivals' shins with!

Greased-up with Vaseline and suitably shoed you are ready to run anywhere, but there are one or two other items you may wish to consider before braving the elements: other bits of gear that might enhance your running experience, and still others that are aimed at giving you scientific information which can actually be used to determine the nature of your training. The classic is the heart rate monitor and it can often be spotted on a fair proportion of dawdlers and striders alike. A fine example is Billy the Wrestler, a portly gentleman, who obviously does not feel the cold as the top half of his normal running apparel consists of nothing more than that thin black strip and wristband that make up the standard **HRM** His man-boobs hanging over the chest-strap look capable of holding enough lactose to bring up Romulus *and* Remus far bigger and stronger than any wolf-mother. Billy's average running speed, indeed his *only* running speed, is around thirteen minutes a mile. Nothing wrong with that at all, indeed I genuinely respect and admire the effort put in by those who finish their races when most of the field is changed and showered and tucking into a second generous slice of sponge-cake provided by the culinary goddesses from the local cricket club. The point is, why does Billy, and by extension why do *you* need a heart rate monitor? By placing your fingers gently against your neck you can easily feel your pulse and check it against your watch if absolutely necessary. If you can't find your pulse like this you are either running fast, have numb fingers, or are clinically dead!

Heart rate can be a useful training tool. There may be sessions when you want to run at your **anaerobic threshold** or when you don't want to exceed a certain level of effort, but it is far from certain that your heart rate is an accurate indicator of either of these things. Caffeine, tiredness, stress and even burping all affect how many beats that pump of ours is squeezing into one minute and the 175 flashing at you from your wrist could well be conning you into thinking you are going a lot harder than you really are. Conversely you may actually be giving it everything and unable to shift that number over 150. Yes, our heart rate can give us useful information but it should not be the defining element of a training session. By all means take your pulse in the morning and if it is 10 beats higher than usual you will know that you *might* be getting ill or are overtired. By all means do a regular run over a set distance at a pre-determined heart rate and use any improvement in speed as an *indicator* of increased fitness. Chances are, however, that you already knew what the **HRM** is telling you. Those of us with a few years of running experience can tell you our heart rate within one or two beats without even checking. The best monitor of all, a completely personalised product with infinite functions and applications, is your brain! Perceived effort is far more useful than heart rate. Don't throw your HRM in the bin, but don't bin your training session because of it either.

These days everything is downloadable and interactive and might even tell you when you need a cup of tea. These **Garmin** GPS jobs are covering the forearms of more and more athletes. Great for measuring distances and average speed, but otherwise they are just excess weight that will slow you down. Those hours spent downloading your data and analysing your performance aren't really going to make you faster, are they? Miles make champions; gadgets just make money for technology companies.

The sad truth is that running, like most things, is a victim of trends and fashions which are largely engineered by global companies with profit, not performance, as their number one priority. Of course research has gone in to providing us with garments that give us greater comfort and protection. Where would be without lovely Lycra for example? Nothing highlights the contours of the generously proportioned more vividly. Gone are the days of gritty northerners running up and down the freezing fells in itchy woollen jerseys. Now we are protected by sweat-wicking, waterproof, windproof, heat-refracting, god-knows-what-ing **Goretex**.

On our noses we sport a nasal strip which supposedly opens up our conks so that we can sniff more air in with every breath, or has that one gone out of fashion now? As for headgear, the baseball cap has given away to the skull-cap, or 'condom' as my training partners laughingly call mine. Not that runners actually need condoms: they are usually either too knackered or too boring to get their leg over anyone except another knackered, boring runner. Am I perchance alienating my readership here? I was only kidding. You are super-studs the lot of you!

Keeping warm when you run and staying warm when you finish is to be recommended if you want to fend off those colds and bouts of flu. With no medical evidence to back me up whatsoever (apparently it's a myth that you lose any more heat out of the top of your head than from anywhere else) I suggest wearing a hat and a top that covers your neck (a neckerchief is a rather fetching alternative). As soon as you get indoors, get in a hot shower (bugger the ice bath) and dry off properly.

Of course, for racing things are different. You want to feel light and move freely but still not at the expense of possible **hypothermia** I proudly look back over photos of me crossing the finish line of a half or even full marathon in long sleeves and a rain-sodden, horribly deformed, Cambridge United (don't go there, or actually *do* go there, they need any support they can get) woolly hat!

After all the negativity in this chapter I feel duty-bound to end on a positive note, and to do so I will sing the praises of the skimpiest of running apparel, the club vest! Too much of this sport of ours is about selfishness and each to his own. It makes a great, refreshing change when we can compete for our club in a relay or other team event that gives us a chance to belong to something bigger than ourselves and feel like we are representing not just the individual under the vest but also the team as a whole or even our town, city or region. Even in training we can feel an affinity for others in the same club colours and feel like we are marking ourselves out as proper runners rather than just fitness enthusiasts. Not your scene? Well don't worry, slap on the Vaseline and let's get back to the loneliness of the long-distance runner.

MILE 5

WALKIES!

It's the first Sunday morning of the new you. Full of determination, you got up early, wolfed down your porridge, put on your favourite running socks and headed for the front door. That is where you are now; you know what it is you want and you want it *bad*. You fill your lungs with three deep gulps of (relatively) fresh air and take your first purposeful strides, letting the door slam shut as you go.

Approximately sixty-eight seconds later, your euphoria has turned to pain and despair. Not through lack of fitness but because a) you didn't give the porridge enough time to go down properly and b) you forgot to pick your keys up off the table and are acutely aware that you are going to ruin your spouse's beloved Sunday lie-in when you press that doorbell on your return. The rest of the run is coloured by this nagging thought and the intermittent stomach cramps. If only you had stopped to think for a minute.

Whether you are embarking on your first ever steps that will involve a point at which both feet are off the ground at the same time or whether you are already a familiar sight on the back pages of your local rag, looking for a way to step up to the next level of distance-running prowess, you have to use your brain. Legs alone can't make you fitter. You have your desire and your target but you need to know *what* to do, right from that first Sunday of the new you.

As I have hinted before, what you don't need is a detailed plan. What you *do* need is a basic grasp of logic and that will tell you that if you train the same then the results will be the same. As you lift your right knee for the first time, stop! Turn left instead of right; do something different! Of course if you are just starting out in running, the mere fact of being out of bed at this ungodly hour already represents the achievement of something radically different.

Our bodies adapt to handle the stresses we put on them and that is what training theory is all about. It's the same with most things! When you start drinking alcohol, a couple of halves of 'disco juice' (weak lager) will render you squiffy, but drink them regularly for a few weeks and you will need four times the amount to produce the same effect. It's the same with getting up early or lifting weights. The more you do it, the more your body adapts and the easier it becomes. Ultimately we want our bodies to adapt to running faster and further. Not a problem for the beginner who can just add a few minutes or miles to their weekly running totals and watch their running performance develop more quickly than a teenager's temper. What do I suggest then for that first, adrenaline-charged Sunday session, the first on the long, hard road to greatness? Please don't laugh or give up on me after you have read the next four words. How about a walk?

This suggestion is not just for those of you who have no choice in the matter as anything more than a dash for the bus is in itself a herculean effort, but for all of you. Walking is seriously underrated. The training logs of Cambridge rowers of the early part of the last century display a belief in the benefits of a twice-weekly 'brisk walk on Coe Fen', but more relevantly there is current research (in particular by the respected endurance coach Bobby McGee) that suggests that all but the very fastest marathon runners (i.e. finishing well under 2;30) could actually improve their times by inserting brief periods of fast walking at regular intervals during the race. The walking brings the heart rate down slightly and utilises different muscle combinations, thereby preserving some freshness in the legs and preventing the drastic reduction in pace which characterises the last kilometres of the great majority of marathon efforts. Maybe you wouldn't be seen dead walking during a marathon (if you were, that really would be a miracle), and that's fair enough. The real reasons I am asking you to start your new regime with a walk are not these.

The walk will gently warm your muscles, it will give you time to think, and in a matter of minutes, it will have you desperate to break into an actual run, which is the best frame of mind to be in to run well. Not only that, your starting point for actual running will not be the usual kerbstone or front gate and this will encourage you to run somewhere different, or a bit further, or at a different pace. Difference means surprising the body, snapping it out of its everyday comfort zone and making the first little move towards adaptation and change into a state of greater fitness. Please, when walking, even at the stage where you are speeding up and itching to break into greater athleticism, do not swing your elbows and wiggle your bum like a race walker. Spare us that sight, I beg of you, or just change sport!

I can't call a chapter 'walkies' and not mention dogs. To many runners the canine is a mortal enemy to be avoided at all costs and it doesn't surprise me that it is these 'antis' who tend to have the bad experiences. In twenty years of running I have never been seriously attacked, although I have had to do some nifty ankle-flicks to liberate my leggings from the gnashers of the odd over-exuberant Jack Russell. This tends to send the wiry fur-balls flying through the air and landing a few metres away with a yelp that, unsurprisingly, angers their human carer. 'Oh well, catch me if you can, mate!' Very occasionally I have felt it necessary to take an unplanned diversion when seeing a path or gateway blocked by a particularly murderous looking Doberman or Alsatian. When out running with a dog-hater it is invariably them that the long-tongued, drooling beasts will make a bee-line for. They must be able to smell the fear and identify these people as easy targets, not only for attack, but sometimes even for attempted copulation with their lower limbs. At the other extreme are the runners who feel the need to be attached to their dogs all the time; in training and, believe it or not, in racing! We now have the sport of, wait for it, **Canicross**! Equipment needed for a five-kilometre race is listed thus: waist-band for humans; connecting 'canix line' to dog; eye protection for dog; harness for dog; booties for dog. The one vital item that is not mentioned is 'straight-jacket', for the humans of course!

Four-legged friends can boost your running in certain cases. As well as giving you an extra reason to get outside, their constant pace variation can give you a hell of a **fartlek** session (more on those later), but if Fido is constantly stopping to mark his territory or is showing that he must have consumed more than his fair share of Pedigree Chum, you will be forced to stop and start and will soon get frustrated. Not ideal either if your canine companion is in worse shape than you or has legs that are only about two inches long. You really don't want to be seen dragging a distraught Dachshund by its neck as you drive on up a hill, desperate to maintain your six-minute-mile pace. Dog leads do not enhance running style. Unless you can hold the lead loosely as you let your arms swing freely in your natural motion, the constant pulling and jerking will put unwanted strain on your neck and shoulder muscles and detract from the poise and balance required for optimum running efficiency.

I have been known to top up my running mileage whilst leading a horse by its bridle but again, mainly for safety reasons this time, I do not recommend it. When it comes to serious training a man's best friend is not his dog, horse, hamster or any other pet, but himself. Man *is* naturally gregarious, however (at least that's what they taught me at school), and just as we liked to hunt in packs, we now (even as enlightened vegetarians) enjoy running with fellow Homines sapientes. Should we resist this temptation too?

MILE 6

HELL IS OTHER PEOPLE

So said the late Jean-Paul Sartre, famous existentialist and distance runner. Who can forget the neck and neck finish of the Café de Paris half-marathon, 1947, when Jonny-boy was just pipped to the line by the great Albert Camus? Absurd and entirely fabricated as this anecdote may be (given that hell is other people, Sartre would have preferred to run on his own anyway), the fundamental concepts of existentialism can actually help us with our training!

Thrown onto this planet without having asked for it, the thinking human being tries to make sense of this life and to somehow give it some meaning. According to these French boys it is only what we actually *do*, as individuals with the capacity to make our own decisions, that can have any significance and meaningfully determine what we *are*. Am I losing you already? Let me put it simply in two sentences: 1. You don't become a runner by sitting on your arse (stating the obvious, I know). 2. You don't become a runner by doing what someone else tells you to do, by following someone else's schedule, or by running at someone else's pace.

Many of us actively despise running on our own or even feel unsafe doing so. A ninety-minute 'long run' on a rainy Sunday morning can go spirit-crushingly slowly as every minute seems to take longer to go by than the last. At every corner we sneak a peep at our watches, hoping, to no avail, for the numbers to have moved on. Eventually we make it home, miserable as sin, vowing never to repeat the experience. Yet of course a week later we are out again, this time with a group of friends, laughing and joking our way around the same route which now seems only half as long.

Finding others to run with should be easier now than ever before. Just about every town in the country has its own running club, either specifically for road runners or a general athletics club which has an endurance section. The perception that these clubs exist solely for 'proper' athletes is now totally unfounded, with the exception of a very few outfits that have been created as a publicity vehicle for their sponsors. You might be unlucky and find a rather snooty bunch who have their own nice little clique that is hard to break into but more often than not us runners are a friendly bunch, certainly much more so than road cyclists who often can't even be bothered to nod their heads in salutation as they pedal by. Membership fees are usually reasonable and with your subscription should come that renowned emblem of acceptance into the wonderful world of athletics, the club vest!

As the recession bites, the move from the **treadmill**, out of the gym door and on to the streets, is gathering momentum and becoming a stampede. Whatever the state of the economy, it makes sense. Why spend a small fortune and waste a shed load of time and fuel getting to the gym, when you can avoid the trashy music, muscle-bound narcissists and blaring TV screens by just stepping out of your front door for a run? Chances are you will burn a lot more calories too! Nevertheless, the gym sometimes offers a nice social side and gives you access to equipment and facilities most of us can't quite squeeze into our loft or garage. Many gyms have a running group that sets off together at a regular time and this can be a good way of getting consistency into your training.

At this rate I'm in danger of convincing myself of the benefits of running in company! I could even go on one of those new dating sites. Yes there's something there for everyone, from 'fitrunningsingles.co.uk' to 'sado-masochistmarathonmatch.com' and beyond. Who knows, you could run your way into lifelong marital bliss. Bleuuuurgghh! Pass the bucket somebody!

If you just want to make running friends then go to your Facebook page, your Gumtree ads or even organise a running **flash-mob**, but if you are in this to actually improve as an athlete you need to think about the effect that being sociable is having on your performance.

Many of you meet your running partner at the same place, say outside the Hare and Tortoise, at the same time of day (it probably suits one of you a lot more than the other), and for the same type of run. You talk about the same things, stating the bleeding obvious about the weather or marvelling at how clubmates have set yet another **PB**. (Who are *they* training with tonight?) Once or twice a week, when one of you is feeling particularly fresh, the pace goes up and you pat each other on the back at the end.

'Bloody good session tonight, eh?'
'Yeah, not half! Same time tomorrow?'
'Okay. Slow one, though!'
'Of course.'

There is a positive side to this too. You commit to being there and you get some consistency in your training, but where is the stimulation? Where is the excitement? Where is the training that will shock your body into adapting to the demands of running further or faster? One of you is probably 'the hare' and your 'tortoise' friend, providing the increase in pace does not cause injury, might learn to scuttle along a little faster. The trouble is that after Aesop's little twosome became friends (the hare soon learnt that it wasn't a great idea to take a nap just before the last mile of a half-marathon) they enjoyed each other's company so much that they always wanted to run together. Instead of the hare becoming more like a gazelle and the tortoise following suit, they both ended up plodding round together like a pair of eccentric ageing rabbits.

Of course, like any romantic liaison, running together can take couples in a variety of directions. Whilst our tortoise and hare ended up, metaphorically speaking, curled up on the sofa together, Jack and Jill had a much stormier relationship! They were much more similar in their ability and both shared a passion for hilly courses. Much as they loved each other, they were only happy when they had beaten their partner to win the latest contest. They trained like nutters and Jack, being slightly stronger, was the most frequent wearer of the hill-running crown. One day Jill gave it absolutely everything, pumping arms and legs like nobody's business, and made it first to the top. As Jack tried one last bound to stay alongside his lover and arch-rival, '*snap*' went his **Achilles**! Yes, you guessed it, Jack fell down and broke his crown and Jill came tumbling after!

Don't worry, I'm not going to start recommending running around the Mulberry Bush or picking on the Humpty Dumpties amongst us. What we all need to be aware of are the dangers and limitations of running with other people. Running the *club sessions* two or three times a week usually leads to an over-emphasis on track and other **speedwork** You never get a chance to construct a solid base of distance work, from which you can then build to a peak (much more on this in later chapters).

The temptation to run in good company can be overwhelming. Even if you start off with noble intentions, it is no guarantee that you will be coming home alone! It's great for running as a sport that there are more people striding their way to fitness than ever but it also means that the chances of you overtaking or being overtaken by some friendly soul who wants to strike up a conversation are pretty much odds-on. It might do wonders for your social life, yet it will *adversely* affect your running. If you are the 'overtaker' you will be taking the easy option by slowing down; if you are the 'overtaken' you will be pushing too hard and suffering the consequences the next day.

Admittedly this is more of a 'glass half-empty' than a 'glass half-full' way of looking at it. I speak from experience, however, and know that getting running partners, just like getting married, can be a damaging compromise or a recipe for disaster. It can lead to psychologically harmful rivalry, jealousy and acrimonious break-ups. Before that, it can develop into humdrum routine and a sense of obligation that is ultimately pointless. For the runner, routine is the enemy of progression. Relationship advice for athletes: 'Just say no!'

Some coaches say that eighty percent of success comes from the brain and it is undeniable that a massive part of running well is down to how strong your mind is. How good are you at getting your head to force your body to move further and faster than its comfort zone dictates? Training with other people either lets you stay in that easy-paced, relaxed tempo that you could experience just as easily in a game of badminton, or, if the other runners are faster than you, it passes the buck to them to push you to that place which your own *mind* should be driving you to. You cannot predict how any race or time-trial will go. Even if you pay a pacemaker, you can't rely totally on their keeping a regular rhythm or, more importantly, on how you will feel inside as you follow behind. There are times when you need to surge, times when you need to relax for a few seconds, times when you have to be alone with your thoughts.

The next chapter is all about what goes on in your head. Whilst not advocating some kind of alien-inspired genetic modifications, two heads (maybe even three or thirty-three) are better than one. There is no denying that we can all learn from other runners, whatever their ability relative to our own. I called this chapter 'Hell is other people' but I know you will carry on training with your mates and so you should. Just make sure it is for the right reasons and not just a cop-out. Remember: 'the waterfall and the strong man channel their *own* path.' That's how they find their little bit of heaven.

MILE 7

NO-BRAINER

'So what do you think about while you're running? Don't you get bored?' To the uninitiated, these seem perfectly reasonable questions. Often they are the same people who don't know how to be happy in their own company, without distractions. They always need to be doing something and then telling anyone who will listen what it is that they have just done. At home the telly is always on, Facebook or Twitter are a must and the iPhone needs constant recharging. When these people start to run they are unnerved by the threat of solitude. Instead of seeking out peaceful towpaths or secluded woodland trails, they prefer to run down the high street or out to the motorway slip-road and back. Not only that, they worry more about the choice of music on their MP3-player and making sure their headphones are properly secured, than they do about how they are running. As a result you see them weaving their way along the busy pavements and polluted roadsides. The music in their ears affects their gait and you see them putting in an unnecessary little skip and doing their best to stop the instinctive head-nodding triggered by such motivational classics as 'Eye of the Tiger' or 'Keep on Running' (yawn, yawn). If they don't change their running habits they soon disappear back into their houses. There is only a certain amount of Survivor anyone can take and if you insist on wearing earphones you won't be a survivor for long! Many race organisers are taking the sensible step of actively discouraging their use or even banning them. If you want to end up under a car I suppose that's up to you, but if you don't hear me coming as I come up behind to lap you, you could stop me getting my **PB**, and that *is* intolerable!

Getting back to those original questions then, and though we might feel gut-twisting, bone-pounding pain and strength-sapping, life-draining exhaustion, *no*, we don't get bored! Things can only be boring if they do not absorb you completely. Boring things tend to be easy, repetitive and no fun. 'Yes, just like running!' you cry. For boredom to exist, however, there needs to be some spare mental capacity that allows your mind to observe what you are doing, as if from outside of yourself, and to make the decision that it is not satisfying or motivating you enough. Running *can* be repetitive and even easy at times but the point is that it should consume you: you and your running should become one and the same. Just as great musicians seem at one with their instrument and live every single note they play, so you and your motion need to become one. That is how you become a 'runner' rather than someone who runs. Total immersion in the movement, the breathing, the discomfort, the terrain, the surroundings, the sound of your feet on the ground and the air rushing past your ears. *That* is being a runner.

It might be worth pointing out at this stage that I haven't got long hair and a beard, I never touch skunk or wacky-baccy of any sort (well, I never inhale anyway), and I don't spend hours sitting cross-legged trying to levitate! There *are* those, however, who have seen running as a path to enlightenment. Perhaps the best known is the spiritual teacher Sri Chimnoy, who even founded his own team and series of races. His main teaching was that 'running means continual transcendence (going beyond), and that is also the message of our inner life'. By setting ourselves new targets, by trying to go further or faster or both, we discover more and more about ourselves. According to 'Sir Sri' (I just liked the look of that), 'competition is good, provided it is the competition of self-transcendence and not the competition of ego-demonstration'. It is at this point, in my macho little Western way, that I start to disagree. Even though it might be shallow and ultimately pointless, boosting your ego every so often feels bloody good and I thoroughly recommend it!

We digress! There we were, totally immersed and at one with our running, and then I start going on about ganja and hairy Hari Krishnas. Let's get back to the key issue of where our head should be as we churn out the kilometres, be it in the pursuit of weight loss, to chase faster times or indeed for the seeking of spiritual enlightenment. Physically speaking, of course, our head should sit pretty still on our neck and shoulders, although some vigorous head-rolling never did Paula Radcliffe any harm and some proponents of the **pose running** method might advocate a slight forward and downward tilt. Needless to say, what's going on inside your head is what really counts and for many of us even the first step we take is already the sign of a victory in a vicious mental battle between 'the dosser' and 'the doer' that cohabit inside our brains. Once on the move we don't want any more battles, we want to relax, to let our thoughts wander, to sweat out the stresses and strains of a day at work or surrounded by the kids. Some of us use our running as an aid to clarity of thought and use this time to try and actively solve the problems we are facing in all walks of life.

All these things are not totally incompatible with the idea of being at one with our running. The run provides the rhythm, different each day and with every type of session, for our thoughts. The endorphins that are released into our brains supposedly give us the increased perception and ability to find solutions, helped and mirrored by the very act of running from one point to another. We get to think more clearly, on a higher level, than we would otherwise. This kind of 'outward focus' allows time to fly by and is to be encouraged on the days when we are not stretching ourselves to the limit. For maximum performance, however, we have to look inside, not out, and use our minds to drill into every little aspect of our running to find the maximum levels of effort that we can hold for the required time. We will look into race tactics later but here we can investigate the types of thought pattern that can give us, some will confidently maintain, an extra ten to twenty percent advantage over our outward-focusing competitors.

The Ultras were a heavy metal band and Chad was their drummer. One night he was feeling rather rocky but the gig had to go ahead. He made it through the energetic two-hour set, right up to the last climactic anthem that was an ever-quickening crescendo of noise called 'Marathon'. (I do hope these names are not leading you to question the veracity of this tale!) He could feel the strength starting to drain from him, but he just had to keep the beat going. The band depended on him. His forearms were starting to burn, he felt like screaming out loud and after a few more bars he did, but the drumming did not stop. Now his fingers were going numb and he could only just feel the drumsticks in his hands. He homed in on what sensation there was left, like when you carry a boiling hot cup of tea to the table and you know you can't let go till you get there. The bass was in danger of leaving him behind as the rhythm quickened again to its final breakneck minute of metal mayhem. Chad was on the verge of collapse; the blood had drained from his face and he felt like each and every downward blow would be his last. He had no idea how his arms were still going up and down. His vision and all his senses were tunnelled towards his fingers. The song had to go on, *he was* the song. Finally the last screeching chord was released and all that was left was for Chad to land that last double-handed blow to the cymbal. With his last milligram of energy he not only brought his arms down but his whole body went plunging into the massive drum-kit, sending stands, sticks and hi-hats flying in various directions. Chad had focused inward. The next day he left the band and took up market-gardening, a happy and satisfied man, forever a legend amongst the Ultras faithful.

When you run you set your own drum-beat. The rhythm will pick up and slow down but if you do not get inside it, if you don't make it fit the music of your thoughts, then the song, the quality of your run, will fall apart. Running is a natural, pre-programmed type of exercise. Created or evolved or a bit of both, most of us are lucky enough to grow up not needing to *learn* how to run. Since the earliest days of humankind, we have needed to escape, to get away fast (this is a relative term of course), and thousands of years of our ancestors legging-it for all they were worth from wild dogs, cannibals or over-zealous Jehovah's Witnesses, have bestowed upon us the gift of being able to run. Unlike riding a bike, or worse still swimming, running comes naturally and this frees up our brain as we punish our heart, lungs and musculoskeletal system.

We can use our thoughts to try and guide our physical performance towards an ideal. Try to have a clear mental image of how you want to look as you run well. Picture yourself striding out, covering the ground with consummate ease! You are beautiful, you are your own Olympic champion. The fact that for the rest of the day you are a shrivelled, old, ugly git, who would benefit from a bag over your head, is irrelevant. Just as important as the picture in your head is the sensation and the thought-stream that accompanies it. If you have ever felt really good when running, hold on to the memory of how it felt and foster and develop that memory each time you try to reproduce it.

The first thirty seconds of a training session will usually set the tone for the whole run. If you feel bouncy and light and full of energy the chances are that you will enjoy it all and have positive thoughts throughout. More common is the scenario where something is aching, you have a bit of a headache, it's raining and the kids in that passing four-by-four have just pointed at you and laughed. This is when you have to use your inward focus to get you on track. Remember that a chain is only as strong as its weakest link and you have to repair it before you can go faster.

Concentrate on the part of your body or the feeling that is bothering you and home in on it. Tell those calf muscles to relax or that pain above your eyes to disappear. Commit to the run and persuade yourself that you will complete it and enjoy it, regardless of how deflated you are feeling right now. It's amazing how many pains just vanish with ten minutes of effort under your belt (thereby rendering you in a fit state for a further ten minutes of under-the-belt action later on!).

Running teaches you about yourself and with experience you get to know the difference between a niggle and an injury, exhaustion and lethargy, the pains that will go and those that will stay. Self-induced pain, the sort that comes from training hard and putting in real effort, is the subject of the next chapter, but those pains that we did not intend to create, even if our actions (such as necking four pints of Stella the night before) have led to their existence, need a different kind of mental strategy. These range from pounding heads down to bruised toes but you know they are staying for the duration and in some way or other you are going to have to grin or grimace and bear them. Here is where the inverted telescope technique comes into its own! Nothing to do with yoga positions or star-gazing, this is a mental strategy promoted by, amongst others, the Italian playwright Pirandello. He advocated coping with life's trials and tribulations by imagining looking in at them through an inverted telescope which makes everything appear minuscule. In the grand scale of things and with the passage of time that which seems so powerful and consuming now becomes trivial and laughable. So next time you are hurting and wondering if you will be able to keep on putting one foot in front of the other, transport yourself mentally to a far away place. Look down at yourself, tiny speck of sand that you are, and laugh at the importance you are giving to what are ultimately minuscule discomforts. Alternatively, use your mind as a TARDIS to travel forward in time; maybe years and years ahead or just to when you will be happily tucking into your dinner that same evening. Think of how your current pain will just be an insignificant inconvenience you can hardly remember that pales into nothingness next to the satisfaction of having achieved your aim.

The accomplished and experienced running mind can be at one with the moving body and hover analytically outside it at the same time. I promise you, it's not only women who can do this kind of multi-tasking. Now, where was I?

MILE 8

NO PAIN, NO GAIN

Don't worry, after this chapter we start cheering up again, being positive and looking forward. We might even agree to start formulating some kind of a plan! Just bear with me for a few more pages of tortured anguish. I told you I wasn't a hippy and I'm not some kind of self-harming 'Goth' or 'Emo' either. (Blimey! Thinking about it I do wear black a lot and I have got a Bauhaus CD.) No, it's okay, I don't walk with a stoop and I definitely don't invert my crosses or hide from the sun.

'No pain, no gain' has become a bit of a mantra for fitness fanatics of all varieties, but the original quote is from a very sedate source, a Quaker called William Penn, who *penned* it whilst in prison in the Tower of London. The full citation gives us a better idea of its true meaning and its wider relevance. 'No pain, no palm; no thorns, no throne; no gall, no glory; no cross, no crown.' To gain a reward which has any meaning, indeed to *give* it any meaning, we have to suffer first. We don't need a religious disposition to appreciate this. If I go out on no training and win the Isle of Arran 10k by beating two grannies and a chain-smoker, that will not give me the same satisfaction, however big the trophy, as finishing the London Marathon in a time only thirty seconds quicker than last year, but which I have only managed to achieve through six months of running myself into the ground.

To get satisfaction from our athletic achievements we don't just need to accept that there will be pain and suffering along the way, we have to actively seek it! Gradually we let it become part of our life and recognise it for what it is, just another physical sensation. Most coaches will tell you that pain is the body's way of telling you that there is something wrong, that you have to listen to it and ease off when you feel it. There is possibly some medical basis to this assertion but ask any elite endurance athlete (a rower, a runner or best of all a cyclist) and you will be told of the need to experience pain and even go beyond it. Some would go so far as to reverse the concept of pain as a negative response. Commenting on a particularly hard stage of the Giro d'Italia (Italy's equivalent of the Tour de France), Mario Corona, novelist and mountaineer himself, said that 'pain is the medicine of life'. The implication is that suffering is not destructive but life-enhancing. Not only that, the sufferance we go through can actually cure us of many of the stresses and illnesses brought on by modern existence and make us feel more complete. I would stop short of saying that greater fitness necessarily equates to greater health, as the athlete in hard training is always running close to that cliff edge, the other side of which represents something steeper than a 'run-down', more of a plummet into a sea of over-tiredness, colds, mouth-ulcers and lethargy. Over-training is a danger, but for the vast majority of you it is under-training and fear of pain that is holding you back.

Pain comes in many forms and all of them can be useful. Even running through the sharp stabs of a knee or foot injury that would be better off rested can furnish us with the kind of mental strength that needs to come into play in those last bitter-sweet miles of the marathon. Then there is the pain which we associate with **interval training**, those lung-rasping last thirty seconds of gut-busting effort at the end of each **rep** that leave a taste of blood at the back of your mouth: that pain that gives you a contorted facial expression capable of winning you any gurning competition. Physiologically speaking, getting used to this degree of strain will improve your body's ability to disperse lactic acid. More important for you as a distance runner, however, is that it will make the intensity of race pace that much more tolerable or even laughably mild in comparison.

Do you remember sitting an exam and getting an essay question which was just the one you wanted? You write and write, unable to get the information down quickly enough. Your wrist and fingers are aching and your head is starting to throb but you know that every sentence is boosting your final mark and the pain is just a spur to keep going. This is the best kind of pain, the pain that you can feel is doing you good and making you stronger with every few yards you cover. You started off easy, maybe you had a bad patch or two when you felt like stopping and then, at last, you felt yourself breathing hard but under control, hurting but loving it. This is the pain that endurance athletes thrive on. Over the years this feeling becomes a girlfriend that you miss when you don't see her for a while (make it a boyfriend if you are a woman or indeed that way inclined). You know that with this particular running companion you are not just exercising, you are *training*. Naturally you can always have too much of a good thing and when you take this girl for granted and expect her to hold your hand all the way home she will dump you in the cruellest of ways and leave you in the gutter. Forget the harshness of an email or text to end a relationship, this baby is far more brutal; in a matter of seconds you will go from superman to a starving street-urchin, barely able to stay upright. You beg for forgiveness as your lover turns torturer and mocks you as your elegant high-knee action becomes a pitiful shuffle and you change direction to take the shortest road home, fantasising that, for the first time ever, your spouse will happen to be driving that way and take pity on you. You know there is no chance and after all *you* left *her* for the other woman and must now pay the consequences. It is true that a little pain will only provide you with a little gain and that major pain can shock you into the next level you so desire to reach but push it too far and, like a jilted teenager, you will find yourself unable to emerge from a listless sulk for at least a week.

The fourth sort of pain is the worst of all and completely different to the previous three. This is the pain of what might have been, the pain of the shirker, the slacker, the idler, the loafer, the slouch and, worst of all, the quitter. For me, this is the pain of the Saturday morning after the extra pint in the pub the night before. The Saturday morning when my friends are speeding round the local **parkrun 5k** and I am reduced to gingerly climbing on my bike and **sitting on the wheel** of the fresh-as-daisies fellow riders, praying that they choose the flat route today. It's the same pain in the afternoon when I turn into a sofa-dweller, seemingly more desperate than usual to consume endless numbers of chocolate HobNobs but having done nothing to deserve even a single crumb.

Before you accuse me of being like a guilt-ridden, self-flagellating religious fanatic, anxious to be absolved of his sins, apply the same idea to other areas of your life and tell me honestly that you would react so differently! Not training properly is like not shaving or not mowing the lawn. You put these things off and then, when you eventually do have to do them, they are twice as annoying as they would have been in the first place. Of course you could become a beardy-weirdy and live in a house surrounded by a mini-jungle, just like you could be a slob for the rest of your life, but if you are reading this the chances are that that is not an option for you either. Not training gives you that feeling you have at work on Monday morning when you get out that report that you should have prepared over the weekend but gave up for an evening of watching *The X Factor* and *Match of the Day*. It's how you feel when you went for an after-work drink instead of making the effort to get to your son's football match. It's not being able to get it together to put your bin out for collection on a midsummer's morning and then having to endure an increasingly rancid stench for a fortnight every time you walk up your garden path. In short it's a hangover, a pain we can all do without which is entirely avoidable with a modicum of will power. If you are the sort of person who is prone to this sort of lily-livered lapse, get tough with yourself, be your own sergeant major. Get your bleeding hair cut and get out of the door. By the left, quick march! Up, two, three, four! Up, two, three, four…

Of course all pain is relative and we all experience it differently to a degree. There are other pains, like hunger and defeat, that we will mention later and which sometimes need to be welcomed. However, we started with a Quaker quote (not rhyming slang for 'porridge oat') so let's finish with an Arab proverb to show us why it's all worth it and to cheer us all up: 'On the day of victory, no pain is felt.'

MILE 9

'SEX & DRUGS & ROCK & ROLL'

Now there's a chapter title to tickle your fancy! None of that pain and effort rubbish, just pure sensual pleasure. Nor am I going to try and tell you that running is better than sex (even if you do the former in good company and the latter on your own), or that to be a true athlete you have to abstain from these three satanic pastimes. Just for now though, pull your pants up, put out that spliff and turn off The Beatles (they're crap anyway).

In the changing rooms, after the half-marathon, John was buzzing, really buzzing, and he would *not* shut up. 'I'm well chuffed with that, man, I tell ya! I was flying! I wish it had been a full marathon. I could have done another lap, easy!' He took off his running vest to reveal a clean-shaven chest, the left half of which was decorated with some Chinese characters. Seeing my raised eyebrows, he was only too keen to elucidate. 'That one means love, the middle one says "peace", and that one is my name in Chinese.'

'Course it is!' I replied with a smirk. 'John is a really common name in China, isn't it?' My race had not gone nearly so well as his and I just wanted some quiet time to think through the reasons why. John was unperturbed or unaware of the tone of my observation and carried on chatting, twiddling as he did so various of the five, six, seven piercings that adorned his upper ear and left eyebrow. 'I ain't been to bed yet, you know!' he announced proudly. 'I was at Fabric, clubbing it all night. Got the morning train back up then my mate gave me a lift here.' This, I had to admit, was truly impressive and I decided to probe a little further. 'Did you have a few drinks as well?' He gave me a prolonged wink of the bejewelled eye and laughed. 'No, just water and a couple of vitamin tablets' (second prolonged wink). Unbelievable! This guy had just done a half-marathon whilst still rattling with ecstasy. Whatever the pills were, he was definitely *speeding*! 'Did they tell you they were doing combined blood and urine tests on all competitors?' I joked. At the same time I exited the changing room to go and get a nice cup of tea and a digestive biscuit.

Let's be honest here. Drugs are still a great unknown and although they may have been around in the world of sporting competition for fifty years or more, we do not know enough to be able to say for certain that any of them are entirely safe. Quite apart from the cheating issue (more on that later), many sporting heroes, from cyclists like Tommy Simpson to athletes like Flo-Jo (nothing proven, I know), have been cut down in their prime as a result of the chemicals they shoved into their body to try and make them go faster or even just to have a good time!

Equally certain is that drugs are rife in sport and that they can give you a winning advantage that thirty hours a week of quality work will never get near. At the serious end of the scale, sportspeople requiring pure strength and speed can transform their bodies into skin-bursting monstrosities through the use of steroids, growth hormones and the like. Shrivelled livers and shrivelled testicles can seem a small price to pay for the social and financial rewards that accompany success.

For many long-distance runners and other endurance athletes erythropoietin (EPO) has been the drug of choice. By stimulating the production of red blood cells it also boosts the oxygen-carrying capacity of the blood, making prolonged effort at a high work rate that much easier. It has only recently been detectable and new variants keep being produced to stay one step ahead of the testers. Most of us have heard the stories of the Tour de France riders having to get up every couple of hours during the night to do some exercise so as to stop their blood turning into a thick soup and clogging up their veins and arteries. Not a nice way to go for those who forgot to reset their alarm!

EPO is prescribed for some very sick people and for some very sick animals. Living, as I did for many years, with a veterinary surgeon, access to this wonder-drug was not a problem, be it in terms of availability, price or even quantity. Is that why 1998 was such a great year for me? Sorry to disappoint, but no scandal here I'm afraid, for I did not indulge at all. Why? Fear. Pure and simple fear. In all honesty I cannot say that noble sporting principles had anything to do with it whatsoever! All you out there, so quick to clamour for the execution, castration, imprisonment or lifetime banishment of these evil cheats, are you really sure that you would preserve your sporting integrity no matter what? Imagine that it were discovered and proven tomorrow that a spoonful of Marmite (you love it or you hate it), taken an hour before a race, was guaranteed to boost your performance by ten percent. The **IAAF** decide to ban it straight away (hardly surprising given that the chairman is allergic to yeast) but *you*, in the wonderful drug testing-free world of amateur road running, have a choice. I have no doubt that during the week leading up to the London Marathon the Marmite tubs would be flying off Tesco's shelves faster than a Kenyan up the Mall. As the effects became better understood and were proven to be without side effects, Marmite's share price would triple and within two years the IAAF would have rescinded its decision and Marmite would have become the 'Official Partner' of British Athletics. Vegemite, on the other hand, is found not to contain the same miraculous properties and goes bust, accompanied by a sharp fall in the Australian medal tally at the World Championships and Olympic Games.

Leaving aside the possibility of undiscovered benefits for runners in everyday foods and leaving aside drugs such as EPO which we can categorise as 'hard stuff', there exist myriad products, available anywhere from the supermarket shelf to the wonderful world of t'internet, that proclaim to be able to give you that competitive edge that you have always been looking for, those few seconds per mile off your times that will make all the difference. Every week you can read about a new one, from turtle blood to bicarbonate of soda, hyped up by the manufacturers and purveyors, creating a new world of fashion with ever-changing trends in supplementation. You will meet runners who swear by these products ('ever since I started taking **L-carnitine** I have never hit the wall') while others will dismiss them completely ('I had a formula 1 engine fitted in my arse and felt no difference') and the truth is clearly somewhere between the two. This is not some kind of physiology journal or even a book that claims to have any kind of scientific merit, so if you really are that desperate or bored (sorry, I mean 'interested'), get your anorak on and go to the library.

My own flirtation with the dark and seedy world of sport-related drugs and supplements extends to the extra cup of tea mentioned in the 'warm up' (I don't like coffee), caffeine-laden gels labelled 'Xtreme' (much more on gels in the chapters on race tactics), and (shock, horror!) a naughty white powder called **creatine**.

Anecdotal as my evidence is, I am certain that this particular stuff lives up to most of what it says on the Maximuscle tub. After only a few days of mixing a teaspoonful of creatine monohydrate (well under the suggested dose) into my orange juice, I started to notice some physical variation. It wasn't as if my jawbone went all Schwarzenegger or that hair started appearing on the soles of my feet, but my T-shirts were feeling tighter across the chest and I was tending to sweat more profusely. They say that the scales don't lie and I put on a kilo and a half in a matter of three weeks, partially due to an apparent increase in water retention. The real change, however, came in what I felt during the **interval sessions** I used to force myself to attend at the local track on a Tuesday night. As well as knocking a couple of seconds off my 400-metre times, I was finding myself able to complete more **reps** and to handle shorter **recovery periods** without getting that breathless. Fantastic!

Or not. The trouble is that drugs fool your body into allowing itself to perform beyond its natural capabilities. The increased training and the accompanying stresses become easier to tolerate mentally and in terms of **cardiovascular** strain but the Achilles' heel is soon found out. In my case it really was my **Achilles** tendon that got very sore and before long my running was more of a hobble, I didn't dare go near a track and Tuesday nights had become football-watching nights, long before I had had a chance to convert my new-found strength and fitness into a half-decent race result. It's a common tale: calves, hamstrings, knees… Something has to give. Stick to that cup of char my friend, that's *my* advice.

No doubt there are such things as safe supplements and some are probably very effective. I'd love to know what mixture of powder and pills some professional footballers have rattling inside them! Compared to what cyclists have to endure, the level of testing that they undergo (peeing in a test-tube every few months) is laughable. Put this together with the rapid changes in physique and fitness that we regularly witness on Match of the Day and it becomes hard to attribute everything to modern training methods alone. Maybe it is due to all that extra-marital bedroom activity they get up to.

Yes, it's time to talk about sex (baby), but not too much as excessive talking spoils the moment, don't you find? Sex makes most of us feel good and whacks up our testosterone levels, though opinion differs on how long this effect might last. So why all this emphasis on abstinence before sporting competition? It is not as if the sex itself is going to wear us out. Maybe as endurance athletes we outperform your average love-maker, but general consensus has it that intercourse only burns an average of

50 to 100 calories. All that just for one HobNob's worth of energy! Perhaps in some cases it is not the sex that does you in but the hanging around all night looking and waiting for it!

From my minor investigation of the topic, it would appear that intercourse before competition will either improve your performance, as found by a recent Israeli study of female runners, or make no difference whatsoever, as shown by **treadmill** tests comparing speeds twelve hours after sex with tests done in periods of celibacy. In summary, no need to go without as long as you don't put too much effort into it! Let your partner do all the work and you need have no worries about scuppering your chances of a **PB**.

The other worry is that you may risk injury as you do your best to re-enact the Kama-Sutra. Quite possibly, from a runner's point of view, excessive hip-thrusting and excessively heavy partners are to be equally discouraged. Injuries usually occur through over-use (you should be so lucky) or from using muscles in a way to which they are not accustomed (much more likely). Indeed as a section of the population, I would confidently wager, runners are amongst the sexually most *under*-active. Why else are they out at the crack of dawn when they could be sharing breakfast in bed with 'all the trimmings'? High levels of training make you tired which means that your libido will suffer also. On the occasions that we do 'get our oats' the residual tiredness from a big mileage week can have the advantage of lengthening the time required to reach a climax, although we don't really get turned on by our partners checking their stopwatches or worse still falling asleep as we revel in the extent of our sexual stamina. **X-training** it may be, but there are limits, surely?

You really need to worry when your erotic dreams start to develop an association with the act of running. The rhythm and movement which running and intercourse share make this a naturally occurring phenomenon, but the problem could get out of hand if the association spills over into your conscious mind.

Men in particular do not want to be aroused as they race through the streets in the briefest and flimsiest of running shorts. I remember a photo of a winner of the **Hawaii Ironman** triathlon crossing the line in jubilation. Unfortunately it was not only his arms that were raised! Luckily, as we run, our body prioritises our heart and lungs over our genitalia and shrinkage is much more common than enlargement.

Just as nymphomania makes for late nights, so does a passion for rock'n'roll, discos, raves, clubs, gigs, medieval choral recitals or even Take That. Despite the experience of our drugged-up half-marathon runner, John, a night out 'clubbing-it' is not the ideal prelude to a successful training session or race. Nevertheless, and despite my recommendation that all runners should bin their iPods *now*, the relationship between runners and rock'n'roll is generally a healthy one. There is no doubt that music can create an atmosphere and lift a mood and this can be a great asset for an event. Even those of us who loathe those long-haired relics had to smile at the sight and sound of Status Quo rocking the start of the Great North Run a few years ago. Part of the beauty of London and other major marathons is the variety of musical accompaniment to be enjoyed or endured as you slog through those 26.2 miles. Not so keen on the jazz or the Elvis impersonators, my personal favourites are the reggae sound-systems that vibrate through your stomach in the belly of south-east London that is Deptford and Bermondsey. Various other races set you off to the overused strains of the *Chariots of Fire* theme music and this is where the cheesiness starts to become too much. The real nightmare scenario, an ever increasing sight at events such as Race for Life, is when you are making your way to the start line only to be confronted with the plastic over-enthusiasm of an aerobics instructor who is exhorting you for all she is worth to join in as she star-jumps and lunges her way through Kylie Minogue and the Sugababes.

It is vital that your running should set the beat for your music and not the other way round. By all means enjoy the sounds but don't let them dictate the rhythm of your legs and feet. Equally dangerous for your eventual finishing-time are both the slow ballad with the unhurried dawdling that it can provoke and the pumping, 140 beats per minute dance music that can cause an acceleration into **oxygen debt** that will be paid back several times over as you crawl the last few miles. Try to let your music be born of the pace your body wants to go at and let it carry you through the harder parts of a race or long run, often the middle section when you are starting to feel the exertion and know you still have a very long way to go. Something with positive lyrics can also prove motivational and beneficial. I would never *choose* to listen to James Brown and yet I often find 'I feel good / I knew that I would / Yeah I fee-ee-eel good' spurring me on as it rings in my ears and gives me an extra spring in my step. It's a kind of full circle of auto-suggestion: my body suggests the song to my mind that in turn plays it back to my body and causes it to adapt to the message of the lyrics. You can try forcing yourself to play this kind of song in your head as you run but if the tunes do not come naturally they are unlikely to have the desired effect.

Music and dancing really come into their own after the race is over. Forget the playing of the national anthem as you stand stiffly on the podium (not many of us will have that experience anyway), I'm talking about the best way in the world to loosen up and help your body disperse some of those waste products that tighten up your aching muscles. Don't drive home then collapse for the rest of the evening into a TV-watching, sofa-stupor. Drag yourself back onto your feet and even if you can't face going out on the town, stick on that radio station that plays a stream of naff eighties classics and make a fool of yourself in your own kitchen, boogying about as you wash the dishes or make the dinner. Take care with boiling liquids but really give it some. It will do wonders for your mood and probably ease the pain of going up and down the stairs the next morning.

To get the best out of a run some of us need stirring or hyping up, while others need our thumping hearts and adrenaline glands calming right down. Choosing the right music can perform this psychological massage in a painless and enjoyable way. A shared car drive to a race can provide an interesting insight into which category we and our travelling companions fall into. If you are covering your ears and cowering in the back seat to get out of the direct line of the speakers and the ear-splitting death-metal guitar thrashing or the window-shattering arias of an opera soprano, chances are that you do not require the same degree of winding up as the music-selector. Sugary-sweet ballads would normally make me puke into the nearest rose garden, but a Sunday morning drive to a **10k** will often be to the accompaniment of Steve Wright's Love Songs on Radio 2. The comments and dedications, as well as the songs themselves, contrast totally with the driven aggression I need to save for my race, providing the perfect overture for what is to come.

So when it comes to sex and drugs and rock'n'roll, don't be a **blockhead** and, if you really have to partake, don't inhale! Do everything in moderation, including moderation itself, of course! If you want to screw yourself up, that's up to you, but don't inflict your habits on me unless you are a particularly beautiful specimen who promises to satisfy me about six hours before competition to make sure my testosterone levels are still elevated and not to make me burn too many calories in the process.

Back in the real world we have failed relationships, uninspiring mass-produced music and a fear of anything the government decides to call a drug. We see frosty marriages, and not much time for anything but work, eat and sleep. In this reality we have to find time for training and make that training count. Let's build a base.

MILE 10

ACE OF BASE

Without a bass line the song falls apart and loses its rhythm; without a base, a foundation, the building collapses. The same can happen to our running if we do not build up our training correctly. The road to a peak performance is often rightly compared to the construction of a pyramid. The taller and safer we want it to be, the faster we want to go and the longer we want our form to last, then the bigger and broader we need to make the base.

In running terms the base represents the number of miles and other **aerobic** fitness work that we put in well in advance of the day on which we want to perform at our best. This builds up over the days, weeks, months and even years of preparation. If you prefer cars to buildings you can imagine that this type of training is putting fuel in the tank of your Ferrari. On the days when we race we burn that fuel, but the more fuel we have and the better its quality, the further and faster we will go.

For the beginner, the first aim of this period of training has to be to build up to being able to cover the required distance. Always, it stands to reason, train for *distance first* and *then* speed. Where is the sense in being able to run fast for three miles if you have another twenty-three to go when you will find yourself walking, not to mention that last 'point two' of a mile, by which time you may well be dragging yourself on your belly towards the finish line. This basic, **aerobic** fitness is exceedingly easy to develop. Day on day almost, as you add another few minutes to your run, you can feel your fitness and stamina building.

Hugo does alright these days as a forty-three-year-old who finishes in the top ten of smaller races. Twenty years ago, however, he was a cocky little sod. A naturally gifted runner, he would come along to the coached sessions our club used to run on the beautiful soft and even grass of a recreation ground. His favourite session was ten **reps** of 400m, during which he would leave everyone for dead and wave to an imaginary crowd as he did so. It wasn't long before he decided to enter the club's own half-marathon. Weeks before the event he was predicting a sub-70-minute finish and telling us all how he was going to 'whip our arses'. The day arrived and so did he, complete with new pair of sunnies and a support crew of girlfriend, family and friends with a 'Go Hugooooo!' banner draped over the railings in the finish straight. No pre-race nerves for H! 'I'm so pumped!' he told me, and I believed him as he shot away on the 'B' of the 'Bang!'. At the one-mile mark he was leading, a big grin on his face apparently. At three miles he was still out there but not extending the gap. From five to six miles he gave it everything as the race completed its first lap of two and passed through the finish area in front of Hugo's little band of cheering followers. He wasn't leading any more but he was still the front runner from our club. At nine miles I passed a wheezing wreck that had developed a strange jerking shuffle, reminiscent of a Peter Crouch robotic-style goal celebration. 'Alright?' I chirped happily. Clearly he was anything but, for he couldn't even force a reply. Hugo walked across the finish line a full forty-five minutes after the winner. He was glad he had his sunglasses on to hide the tears of pain and humiliation. A few weeks later rumours spread that he had taken up mountain-biking and it was well over a decade before he graced us with his presence at the recreation ground again, by which time his arrogance had been replaced by humility.

   Hugo had trained for speed and not distance. He had failed to build a base and the Windsor Castle that was to be his performance, collapsed dramatically into a pile of ugly rubble on the outskirts of Slough. Just like the kids who learn a thousand fancy tricks with a football but get puffed out running from one end of the pitch to the other will never get to play for the best teams, so the athlete who relies on and cultivates nothing but speed will never fulfil his or her potential as a distance runner. Base training is the cake and speed is the icing on top. Many great cakes don't have icing on them, but icing without a cake can give you nothing more than a sweet, finger-licking moment that leaves you empty.

The benefits of base training never stop. It is just as important to the marathon world-record holder as it is to the pensioner recovering from a quadruple heart bypass, for whom five kilometres is 4,900 metres further than what they are currently capable of running. Top distance runners regularly cover over 100 miles a week and the vast majority of this is steady or base training, well below race speed. So what's so good about it?

As we run more and more without ruining our form by having to strain to go fast, our bodies gradually adapt to a more and more efficient way of covering the ground. Efficiency leads to a lower energy consumption for every unit of distance covered. This means that for the same effort we can move further. As we continue to train our style changes, becoming not only less wasteful but also more aerodynamic. The less surface area we present to the wind by keeping our action streamlined, the faster we travel. We all have our little peculiarities (some less little than others), from head-nodding to elbow-flicking to waving our hands like paddles, but experienced runners are immediately recognisable by the apparent ease with which they move. Unlike new runners with their needless **dishing** of the feet and exaggerated **knee-lift** a hardened athlete will look slower than they actually are whereas the virgin runner gives the opposite impression. Typically, a runner with a good base of training behind them will look very level from the side. In other words, if they were to run along the other side of a low wall, with only the top half of their bodies visible, it would look as if they were sitting on a motorbike with little or no vertical variation. The novices, on the other hand, bounce up and down, often going as high in the air as they do forwards.

Remember that the whole point of training is to increase or vary the load and strain we put on our body so that it will adapt to make that same effort easier to handle and enable us to reach the next step on the ladder towards optimum fitness. For this reason, base training should be progressive. Not necessarily day on day or even week on week, but certainly we should be able to trace our average mileage over any given period of time onto a graph and see the best-fit line pointing well above the horizontal. Building base mileage is the key to the door of success. Nearly every runner I know would improve just by putting in progressively more base miles. So once we have gone beyond just being able to cover the required distance, how should we go about tailoring that training? How do we avoid injury and how do we know when to stop?

If you are going to take your running seriously you should log your runs, or in other words, keep a training diary. In my case these started off as school exercise books with the dates written in the margin and just one line of microscopic biro-scrawl for each day. As I started getting more into my running and then took up triathlon, this became blatantly insufficient and I began to create my own diary designs based on others I had seen. These were an amalgam of badly ruled columns and boxes with space for entering heart rate, weight, perceived degree of effort, and size and texture of my stools (only kidding, but I did consider it!). My advice is to keep things simple and the internet provides us with a plethora of suitable and downloadable training-diary templates to choose from. The essential is to have space for the time and distance of each 'outing' and for weekly totals. A box for other types of training and one for comments on the difficulty, terrain and nature of demanding runs are also recommended. From week to week you can compare your efforts and then in a few years' time you too can be a sad old git and look back at those glory days when you were yet to discover your limits. Believe me, you will spend many more hours perusing the pages of your running diaries than you will looking back on any angst-ridden jottings that you scribbled down, thinking you were being so 'deep', last time you thought you were in love.

Base training is all about increasing the load on your body to make your running more efficient and to make you fitter. The key elements are to increase your total weekly mileage and to increase the distance of your longest run. You may also wish to supplement this with other types of training, which we will look at in the next chapter. Within a few months you will be running 150 miles a week with a longest run of four and a half hours and enhancing this meagre amount of effort with a daily swim, circuit sessions and a cycle to work with a backpack full of bricks. On the other hand, if you happen to be human and happen to have other things in your life apart from running, you will have to plan carefully to find the time to augment your training time at all. The question of how far to push things and how long to run for is nevertheless a very valid one. Each of us responds differently to physical strain, how boring life would be if we didn't … running, and life, would be one long **dead heat**. Vive la différence! Indeed, but some general guidelines can be given.

Clearly you need to avoid grinding yourself into the ground so that you are physically unable to complete your next planned run. You do, however, need to break your body down that tiny bit so that it will repair itself stronger and faster. A reasonable idea is not to increase your training by more than ten percent week on week and to have at least one week in four when you don't increase it much at all. If you operate on a ten-day or fortnightly schedule, the same applies. Bear in mind the intensity of your runs as well as the overall distance covered. You could give each run you do a mark out of 20 made up of a mark out of 10 for distance and 10 for intensity. It is the total of all these marks out of 20 that you add up at the end of the week to give you a total and it is to that number that you should apply the 'no more than ten percent' rule. See? Running can also be brain-training as you do the mental maths to see how your total is progressing and how near you are to surpassing last week's score. It's a great motivator too and you will rightly smirk with smug satisfaction as you boldly circle that crucial number. It will become a highlight, that Sunday evening moment, as you enter your total and turn back the diary pages to view your steady progression.

Remember this is *base* training and the focus is on distance rather than speed. For this reason, increasing the duration of your longest run is one of the easiest ways to build up your all-important total. Despite the lack of pain, the long run does wear you down and anything over about nine miles takes some recovering from. By all means build well beyond this distance but, once you do so, bear in mind the distance you are training for. Running for over two hours as training for a **10k** or less seems counter-productive. In any case, once a fortnight is plenty for a run of that length. Half-marathon training might involve one or two runs of fifteen or so miles and marathon runners may even go up to their full race distance, but this is by no means necessary. Remember the afore-mentioned Cravatta and his regular three-hour tours of the county? Yes, he does well, but he is often injured and is not structuring his base properly. Much more effective than adding and adding to that longest run, is to insert an extra, shorter run during the week or to add a little bit to the medium-length runs.

It won't be long before you notice some positive changes. You may well notice your resting heart rate decrease. We all have points during the day, often late morning or early afternoon, when our metabolism seems to slow down and our mind wanders to a vision of curling up for a nap in our favourite armchair. At these times place two fingers on the inside of your wrist and take your pulse. The first time you do it you might get a rush of adrenaline when you think your ticker might have given up its ticking. Then a strong beat comes through your fingertips and you realise that you are not dead but *fit*! The adrenaline speeds the pump up a bit but you can soon develop a Buddhist monk-like technique to minimise your **BPM** (beats per minute). See if you can beat my record of 28! If you get under 20, not only will you have a better engine than the legendary Tour de France winner Miguel Indurain but you will probably look in the mirror and discover that you are actually a horse!

Don't expect this new regime of base training to transform your physique and make you the Adonis of the office, pursued by a cacophony of wolf-whistles at every step. Extra running will make you extra hungry and you probably won't start shedding the pounds until a few weeks in when your body realises this new craze is not just a blip or an advance warning of a famine that it needs to store up fat reserves for. As you do begin to tighten your belt to that next hole, much more likely than comments of the 'Wow! You look good!' variety are such de-motivating gems as 'Have you been ill?' or 'Blimey! You look tired.' As you notch up those ever-increasing weekly totals, stretching your arithmetical sharpness and inner honesty ('maybe I could rate that one as an 8 not a 7 to get me past last week's total') to the limit, you *will* feel tired. No amount of ginseng tea or Coca-Cola Zero (yuk) can fend off fatigue for good. You will want to snatch and relish every moment of rest possible. You will spend a lot less time on your hair and make up and as for you ladies, you will notice how often you cut yourself shaving and fall asleep during *Top Gear*. You will arrive for work at one minute to nine (on a good day) and forget your daughter's birthday. After all there was a hilly eleven-miler to do that day. The only way to put the phone down will be by slamming it, you will not bother to rinse bottles or tins before recycling them and the extra fiver for online supermarket shopping might seem a good idea after all.

Gradually, however, you will acquire a healthy glow to counterbalance the entrenched, haggard scowl on your drawn features. 'Have you been on holiday?' they will ask, unaware of the tanning effect of the repeated facial battering of good old British rain, sleet and wind. There will be days when you will surprise yourself with the spring in your step. The ease with which you bounced out of the car then nipped through a door in front of someone, when before you would have given way, will make you smile and laugh out loud. Running too, you will have good days. Days when it seems too easy, when your body seems to be doing this running thing for you instead of resisting it at every stride. There will be 'float days', windless and fresh, when you become the athlete you wanted to be and pity the rest of the world for not feeling like you.

Before we get carried away on this current of poetic eulogising, let us remember that most of the time training is like a daily battle against a deep-rooted tendency towards 'slobdom', our body's desire to take the path of least resistance. Sometimes even in battle there has to be compromise and a good basis for starting negotiations with your lazy side is to say, 'We'll just start running and then see how it goes. If I turn out to be too tired to do much, then so be it.' On the overwhelming majority of occasions you will get some enthusiasm up and more often than not a decent session will emerge from the mire of lethargy in which it started. There are times when you have to shock your body into action with some unplanned effort at speed but base training is all about keeping it steady and building up the miles.

I've never really understood why people need to ask what pace they should run at during this type of training. I have always found that my body dictates to me the velocity at which my steady runs should progress. Levels of tiredness and an awareness of roughly how long I need to keep going for and of what training there is still to come in the following days combine subconsciously to programme my legs to turn over at the desired rate. Possibly that just doesn't happen for some people and they need to be *told* how fast to go. Maybe they think it is necessary to operate at optimum fat-burning speed? Certainly the *proportion* of fat burnt per mile increases at a slower pace but over any fixed distance the overall energy used is always more or less the same.

If you build up your overall mileage and long runs and don't compensate with a diet of full English breakfasts and Black Forest gateau you will *necessarily* start to burn off the blubber. Your body wants to utilise sugar first and then fat before it starts chewing up your muscles and vital organs. The long-distance stuff, whatever speed you go at, will turn you into an ever more efficient, eco-friendly smart car of a fat-burning machine.

Still not sure how hard to set off? Well, start easy and build to what feels like a rhythm you can keep up for the longest time you had considered running for. Unless you are an absolute beginner or doing one of those 'brisk walks' we recommended in the 'Walkies' chapter, you should not be going so slow as to be able to check the calorie content on discarded chocolate-bar wrappers as you go along. Nor would it be very sensible to mount an attempt to set off the flash on your local speed-camera. Stop worrying about being too slow or fast and just 'shut up and run!'

Monitoring progress during this phase is relatively easy. One week you spend the last mile sucking in air like a child who is desperate to get that last drop of lemonade up through a straw. The next week you finish the same run with lips barely parted, thereby displaying your feeling of untroubled comfort to anyone who can be bothered to look or has the experience to understand. If you have such a thing as a regular loop, you will have days when you are heading for home and suddenly decide to take a left or even double-back on yourself because you actually feel the *need* to run some more. On other days you will look at your watch and do a double take, unable to believe that after what had seemed like little more than an easy stroll you have sliced a chunk off your previous time. Of course the more experienced a runner you are the smaller those chunks will be: that is the unfortunate law of diminishing returns which eventually dictates the impossibility of anyone ending up running faster than the speed of light and then actually finishing a run before they started it. For the more scientifically minded amongst you, no doubt poised with your latest touch-screen heart rate monitors, there is a very simple test to evaluate your progress. Simply select a two-mile section of flattish road and run it whilst keeping your heart rate at as constant a level as possible, somewhere around 75 percent of your maximum. Record the exact time it takes you to complete the distance and then repeat the procedure at two- or three-week intervals, making sure that you do not exceed the previous attempt's heart rate level. If you are training well you should find that your times get quicker without any quickening of the pulse and therefore, by implication, with an equal level of effort. The presence of a force nine gale or homicidal hoodies forcing you to cross the road will render the comparison somewhat meaningless so do choose your trial venue and timing carefully!

Since the move away from the fashion for high-mileage training which preceded the **Seb Coe/Steve Ovett era**, the majority of coaches and commentators have failed to stress the obvious benefits of base training and give it due importance. Not so in other sports such as swimming, where for the sake of racing what might be a maximum of 200 metres, well over ten thousand daily metres of base training are churned out as a matter of course. Cyclists too will knock out repeated, lower-back-torturing rides of six or seven hours to give them that massive base from which to build a season of successful racing. Running, being a weight-bearing, joint-pounding form of exercise, imposes its own time limits upon us. Though there are those few extra-terrestrials who regularly compete in 100km or even 24-hour events, most of us mere mortals soon find that there is a limit which our body imposes on us, beyond which fatigue and injury are sure to occur. Yes, push your limits, but not to the point of snapping totally. In our quest to train our **cardiovascular system** to the max, we can make up for the inability of our knees and hips and ankles to take any more by jumping on our bikes, diving into the pool or even heading for the ski slopes! Get cross!

MILE 11

MIX IT UP!

Cross training has become the new buzz word (or more accurately 'buzz phrase') in sport over the last twenty years or so. Everybody is at it! Baseball players are throwing the javelin, Australian rugby professionals are learning Judo, tennis players are doing their knees in on the squash courts, boxers are learning to dance and F1 drivers are doing triathlons. Most obvious of all, however, is the newly instated requirement for premiership footballers to spend one month learning to dive with Tom Daley and to spend another three at a leading drama college. Of course all of the above sports use running as a type of cross training too. So where does that leave us athletes and should we bother with it at all?

There is no doubt that the best training for running is to run. The specificity aspect is pretty obvious. You don't learn to paint by playing the guitar, even if both require us to use the wrist. Running, as we have mentioned before, teaches our body to refine our action so that we become more efficient the more we do it. Unless, that is, we already have some muscular imbalance or skeletal peculiarity that causes us to tend to a gait that is far from efficient or even, at worst, damaging to our musculoskeletal system. This need for correction is the first of many reasons that we might consider for indulging in other activities to get us running at our best. Jamie is an ex-footballer with a right leg which is clearly more muscular than his left and he used to run with a bow-legged action. You could pass one of those hula hoops (the plastic rings, not the crisps) between his legs as he ran along. With the help of a (very expensive) personal trainer, Jamie now runs a lot more upright after a good year and a half of **core conditioning** and weight training targeted at redressing the imbalance.

I don't want you to get the impression that cross training is just a cheap alternative to corrective medical surgery. I have no hesitation in advocating it for all of us, whether or not we have the *cross* of a physical impediment to our running to bear, and whether or not we are forced into it by injury or simply the lack of opportunities to run. Nothing is worse than feeling like going for a run but being stuck in a meeting till late on the top floor of a hotel in a strange town whose drivers seem to treat runners as a sub-category of potential road-kill. The other classic scenario is being caught out at work or away from home without proper running kit. On these occasions it is usually possible to cobble together enough semi-suitable apparel to be able to sneak into the gym and hide on a machine with your back to everybody or at least to lock yourself in a room and do some basic **body circuits**.

Although the actual process of putting one leg in front of the other in a running action requires a precise set of muscles to move in a given way, the engine behind them (or more accurately *above* them) consists of our heart and lungs. The 'fitness' of these organs (which is reflected in such things as our **anaerobic threshold** and the **stroke volume** of our hearts) can be improved just as effectively through sports other than running, thereby giving benefits which are directly transferable to our chosen sport. Any sporting activity that elevates our heart rate above about sixty percent of its maximum and maintains it there for more than a few minutes cannot fail to help tune or upgrade our engine, and all without putting extra miles on the clock. The degree of 'transferability' varies greatly when it comes to the actual movements involved. When we go on to look at the individual possibilities we will see how some can give you the feeling that your legs are spinning along faster than ever before, while others convince you that those same limbs have been replaced by 50kg bags of cement.

As we have hinted already, cross training can be a matter of choice and not just necessity. As we augment our weekly mileage and even more so as we introduce races and demanding sessions into our training schedule, the attraction of a day off (or at least half a day for the real mileage junkies amongst you) from giving our fragile pins a weight-bearing hammering on the road becomes more and more obvious. Not only does cross training give our aching running muscles a well-deserved rest without any concurrent loss of fitness, but more than that it can provide us with badly needed mental respite. When you start to worry about your running and find it affecting you in the same way as stressful aspects of your work, it is a sure sign that it is time for a change of scene in your theatre of training.

The principal risk as our pre-programmed legs are forced to escape from their metronomic regularity, ingrained by steady run after steady run, is, of course, injury. My left ankle is still, six years on, weaker than my right one after that fateful morning when I sprinted after a hockey ball, mistakenly trod on it and then heard the crunch as I tore through my ligaments. My feet were used to moving in straight lines in a never-ending attempt at getting from A to B by the quickest route possible and a violent thrust to the side was completely alien and more than I could take. Such was the pain that I had to endure the acute embarrassment of being carried off the playing fields, sack of potatoes-like, by another PE teacher. Unsurprisingly the classes of 15- and 16-year-olds, now unsupervised, decided to invent their own variation of the noble sport of field-hockey and shortly afterwards I was joined in the 'medical room' by a boy with a couple of cracked ribs. Having made the mistake of scoring a goal, his fellow players had shown their appreciation by turning him into a sort of human piñata, beaten till he cracked!

Sports like football, rugby and hockey, wonderful as they are (arguably more fun and certainly a lot more social than running), have to be seen as a runner's worst enemies. What you might gain in agility and sprint-speed is more than offset by the likelihood of you spending half the winter nursing an injury that stops you running at all. Less threatening, yet not without risk, are sports such as cricket and golf and racket sports like tennis, squash and badminton. These usually avoid the obvious dangers posed by 'contact' sports of being tripped, flattened or crushed by a member of the opposition. Nevertheless, even badminton can result in a nasty fall and all sports tend to leave us sore if we are not used to doing them regularly. A few overs bowled at medium pace for the first time that year will leave most recreational cricketers with a sore back and shoulders for the best part of a week. These sports also tend to involve a lot of standing around, which can actually tire the legs more than a run and thereby defeat the original purpose of the activity. If you do go down the route of indulging in ball sports, do some proper stretching and make sure you warm up and down *very* thoroughly.

The local pool, if you can get there when it's open and it has not been hijacked by gangs of screaming 'bombers' jumping in off the side, or by the local swimming club with its hordes of tumble-turning swimming snobs, is a cheap alternative to the gym. Gym pools are often little more than glorified paddling pools that are maintained at stupidly high or low temperatures and are inhabited by breast-stroking old ladies that make octopi look efficiently aerodynamic. We'll come on to swimming itself in a moment but the pool can also be used for **water running**. This replication of the running movement whilst treading water can be performed with or without a special belt that keeps you afloat. An excellent, specific method of cross training for runners of all abilities, **water running** encourages you to pump your arms and lift your knees. You may find yourself moving slowly forwards as you drive those limbs up and down, studiously ignoring the curious stares of the swimmers who are wondering if you have invented a new type of stroke. Embarrassing it may be but its value is unquestionable. A very talented 1500-metre-runner friend of mine injured his heel mid-season and his coach had no hesitation in setting him a full programme of sessions in the water. From long runs to intensive **interval sessions** and even sprints, the workouts he should have done on the road and track were reproduced in the pool. No fitness was lost and Marc went on to set a new personal best later that season.

When you watch a proper swimmer dart up and down the fast lane you see a beautiful ease of movement that carries their body on top of the water with a minimum of splash and in fifteen or so arm rotations the twenty-five metres of the pool have been covered and the next tumble begins. In jumps the runner and the mini-tsunami begins. Arms whirl round and crash in to the water, the head bobs up and gulps in the air before narrowly missing smashing into the far end of the pool. The real give-away, however, is in the legs. For the first few yards an exaggerated kick brings up a washing machine-worth of froth that blinds the swimmer behind and then the 'runner's legs syndrome' sets in! Where the club swimmer was horizontal the runner battles away with the lower half of his body at a 45-degree downward angle to the top half. With the exception of those triathletes who are just swimmers who have added running to their repertoire, there is no getting away from it: runners' legs are dense, they are made of lead, they just sink! Yet swimming is a wonderful recovery session for us leaden-legged lot. The water massages away our soreness and simultaneously strengthens our core. Backstroke, breast-stroke, freestyle (and even butterfly if you have the strength) all give a whole-body workout that may eventually give us some pectoral muscle-tissue and a more athletic shape than the wizened prunes that we evolve into if we do nothing but run. Of course, as with any activity that involves strength work of some sort, we do not want to compromise any fitness gains by putting on extra muscle that can only slow us down. Best then to avoid shoulder-busting sprints and swimming front-crawl with hand-paddles that increase resistance.

Beware the hunger pangs that follow you out of the pool and linger in your stomach for hours or until you satisfy them with copious amounts of chocolate, filled bread rolls, cakes, or all three! Nothing is quite like swimming, despite the relatively few calories per minute that it burns, for making you feel famished.

The calorie-counting thing can become obsessive and we will talk more about nutrition in due course but it is interesting and can prevent us from feeling like we have achieved just as much by riding our bikes or dipping in the water as we would have done on our usual run. This could be a good point to introduce the concept of the **running equivalent.** It is a way of equating time spent and distance covered in other sports with a particular running mileage. Forget stretching, racket sports, mud-wrestling and pram-pushing, but we *will* allow you to up that weekly total we mentioned in the base training chapter if you have done some continuous swimming or cycling. Totalling up the calorie consumption figures is useful when deciding how many plates of pasta you can push past your epiglottis but is not the whole answer. If we take Fred, a forty-year-old male weighing about 75kg as our example, we can see how the three sports match up. In an hour of road cycling at about 15mph, Fred burns about 800 calories on a hilly course. He cools off with an energetic hour-long session of front crawl, holding his own in the fast lane but only burning 650 calories in the process. He walks out of the pool, but only after falling foul of that evil red and grey temptress known as the vending machine, at which he wolfs down a Bounty bar and a bag of crisps, sinks a carton of orange juice and thereby completely replaces the energy value he has just splashed away. Feeling guilty he forces himself out for a solid sixty minutes of running at an average speed of 8 miles an hour. Calories burnt running? 960!

Equating swimming with running puts you on dodgy ground or indeed in dodgy water as the sports are so different, but if you are desperate and are genuinely using your pool time to enhance your running fitness I will allow you a three-to-one ratio. That is to say, an hour of front crawl (not including the rest time in the shallow end when you take a drink and chat about the weather) gives you the same points as twenty minutes of steady running. Believe me, that *is* being generous!

Running and cycling have gone hand in hand (or foot in foot) for many decades now. The sports of **duathlon** and cyclo-cross combine the two forms into one exciting competition. The occasional top runner has made a successful transition to cycling but much more common is for the ageing professional rider to dump his bike and marvel at the ease with which he can destroy the field in long-distance running races. This is not always the case and occasionally the bulging quadriceps and tight calves just won't cope with the change. Remember, however, that cyclists are used to spending very long periods of time in the saddle with their hearts pumping their way to maximum **aerobic** fitness. They are used to surges in effort, to hills and to sprints. If they are then capable of relaxing and straightening their backs a little, they usually run like the wind. You might now be thinking that all this is jolly good for them, but how does it help *me*?

The beauty of cycling is that after an initial period of getting used to it, you can ride for a much longer time than you can run, which is fantastically beneficial for your endurance potential. If you are training for a marathon you can intersperse your long runs with even longer bike rides and get a very similar training effect. Whereas with swimming I allowed you a three-to-one ratio for **running equivalence**, when it comes to cycling you only have to do double the running time. A three-hour cycle therefore equates to a ninety-minute run. You can even go mad and do five- or six-hour outings without suffering nearly as much as you would on a steady run of any more than half the duration.

Come home and have a shower then relax for the rest of the day, safe in the knowledge that you would have to do some serious face-stuffing to rebuild that roll of fat that the ride has melted off your midriff. As you read this the metaphorical relationship danger alarm should be screeching and flashing its lights for all that it is worth. Five hours is a long time for your partner to wait for a breakfast in bed that you spill all over the stairs, too tired to walk up them properly.

I have always maintained that cycling helps your running but the opposite is certainly not true. Go for a hard run the night before a hilly thirty-miler and you may well feel like someone has attached a bag of bricks to the back of your racer when you weren't looking. Running makes your legs feel sluggish as you turn the pedals but this feeling can be minimised if you **spin** an easy gear and lift yourself freely in and out of the saddle to vary your position. Every now and then you can wobble your legs about, stand on the pedals to lower your heels, and curve your back in various directions to stay loose. Turning your legs over at a speed (**cadence**) higher than that at which you normally run is vital. Don't get in the habit of churning your legs round slowly against a gear that mirrors the kind of effort you put into each stride of your run. I have to put my hands up to being guilty of this one: to avoid it is a case of resisting our subconscious tendency to find a comfort zone, which in this case is the feeling we are used to from our steady runs. Cycling is different and to maximise its benefits we need to keep it different. Change those gears (they are there for a reason), don't feel guilty about chatting as you pedal along, attack the hills and sprint for the village signs. These things are what make cycling fun and at the same time can give you an extra dimension when you abandon the frame and wheels for your legs and feet. As you develop the Lance Armstrong that was lying dormant inside you, use your imagination to combine two-wheel and two-leg training to your advantage.

The first time that you ride a bike hard then try to do the same with your running as soon as you dismount, chances are that you will get something of a shock. Duathletes and triathletes have variously described the jelly-limbed feeling as a sensation of 'being given somebody else's stumps to run on', 'dead legs', and 'tree trunks rooted to the road'. Part of this originates from using too hard a gear but mostly it is just a case of needing to accustom your body to the change-over. During the winter you can use a mountain bike and intersperse a few minutes of riding with a few of running along with the bike. Better still, you can swap with a partner who rides alongside when you run. In the gym you can swap to and fro from the exercise bike to the **treadmill**. (Ah the evil, shin-splinting deceiver that she is!) 'Deadmills', as I prefer to call them, are notorious for buggering up your calves and shins. They also tell you that you are running a lot faster than what you are really capable of. Even with the one or two percent gradient that some coaches tell us will make them equate to the road, you will still be flattered. Three kilometres in nine minutes on the rolling carpet will, optimistically, give you a ten-minute finishing time on the track or road. Why not replace a long run with part-run and part-bike, remembering to extend the total time of the workout? It won't be long before the heaviness that you felt the first time is replaced by a wonderful springiness in your step. Indeed a few minutes **spinning** at a high **cadence** works as a great warm-up for a running race. The first couple of miles fly by as your legs seem to take care of themselves, wanting to turn over at a rate closer to that at which you were pedalling. After a race too, when the thought of more running is anything but appealing and yet you are way off reaching your desired weekly mileage, a leisurely ride is just the ticket to round off the week and pull up your **running equivalent** total. This is particularly gratifying after you have put in a pleasing performance. Involuntarily you nod and smile at passing motorists and struggle not to appear condescending or dismissive as you cruise past the

Sunday afternoon cyclo-tourists, wave and call out 'lovely day, isn't it?'.

I am not aware of any other form of cross training that is as beneficial as cycling to the distance runner. I include **spinning** classes here: the 'bikes' used are usually quite hard to set up in a decent cycling position because the saddle resembles an armchair and for anyone with a longish torso it is positioned too near to the handlebars. After three-quarters of an hour of enduring your instructor's idea of what constitutes motivational music (No! Not Roy Orbison's 'I Drove All Night' again, please!), you then have a lovely pool of sweat to clear up and a machine to wipe down and lug back to the store room. A perfect occasion for pulling a neck or shoulder muscle. By now it is well past eight in the evening and you supplement your pre-exercise snack with a quickly prepared, massive bowl of pasta and then have trouble getting off to sleep.

Rowing will give you an admirable physique and punish you as you gasp your way through a 5,000m **ergo** test. When I started rowing at college I was firmly put in my place by the so-called 'boatman' who repaired our beloved vessels and did a bit of coaching from the towpath. In the boathouse itself the dreaded **ergometers** were lined up. Their displays tell you your speed per 500m and the clock counts down to zero after you set your workout time, which in this case was a meagre, novice-friendly six minutes. At university fresh from nine months labouring on a building site and following a strict exercise regime of a hundred press-ups every morning, I thought I would make mincemeat out of this posh-boy sport with its silly machines on which you had to just pull a chain in and out to make a flywheel whir round. I got stuck in, determined to trounce the scores of the two pale-faced lads who had gone before me. The last ninety seconds went on for ever. Every muscle in my body was screaming at me to stop, I was tasting blood and unable to get enough air to my lungs. When I finally saw that long-awaited row of zeros in the time-remaining display, I let go of the chain, which slammed against the machine, thereby attracting the unwanted attention of the aforementioned Mr Unsympathetic, the boatman. I rolled off the **ergo** in agony, eyes screwed shut, squirming on my back as if in the throes of ecstasy. 'What do you think you're playing at?' shouted the nasty man. A full sentence was beyond my capabilities but I held up six fingers and forced out the words 'six minutes' as if they were describing the achievement of the decade. With a curl of the lip and a smirk, I could tell that my admonisher was far from impressed. 'I do forty minutes every night and I don't treat the machine like that, ever!' From that day on, long before I took up running, I had a deep respect for all endurance athletes. As I moved up the rowing ranks Mr Unsympathetic was renamed Paul and became a friend. When I see him out running I like to make sure that he knows I have done my daily forty minutes!

Boxing will give you excellent conditioning and might help you rediscover that you do in fact possess abdominal muscles. A small price to pay for possible brain damage, don't you think? If you miss out the conflict element, crucial to the boxer though it may be, you are left with a punishing regime of skipping, medicine balls, **body circuits** and bag-punching that will make the pain of a long run that much easier to bear. Again we do need to be careful not to get worn out by it and those of you lucky enough to be so young as to have an abundant supply of testosterone still running through you, also need to be wary of not bulking up.

At the end of the day, as football pundits never cease to repeat, we are judged by our results and the same approach should be taken to cross training. If you have been pedalling, punching or paddling for months on end and are finding your running times getting slower instead of quicker, now is the time to change your cross-training habits. Running, like the league in football, is what you have to save the most energy for and devote the most time to. Let the other sports be the equivalent of the Auto-Windscreens Shield or some other minor competition for which the big teams bring out their youth players and rest the important ones. If you have the health, the energy, the time, the location and the disposition to run then do so. Cross training is for when one or more of these elements is lacking. Don't get caught up in it so much that it becomes another type of competition and an extra mental stress. If cross training is making you cross, then cross it off your list!

MILE 12

YOU RUN WHAT YOU EAT

'You are what you eat.' However did that phrase gain any credence? Most of what you eat comes out the other end. Maybe that really is all we are, a big lifetime's heap of faeces, but *faeces don't run* (great name for a band?) and anyway, nihilism gets you nowhere! The element of truth in the phrase lies in the fact that the kind of food and drink that we ingest can affect our physical, mental and emotional wellbeing. Consequently, and given that food is our primary source of energy, there is also some truth in our little adaptation which reads 'you run what you eat.'

I adore fry-ups! Admittedly my version of a moral code only allows me the veggie version, but there is little I prefer to a plate overflowing with hash browns, veggie sausages, baked beans, mushrooms, grilled tomatoes (is your mouth watering yet?), at least two fried eggs, veggie bacon and fried bread. The one plate is not enough of course, as a side-platter is required to hold the heavily buttered toast and fresh bread. Add to this the steaming, pint-sized mug of tea, the squeezy bottles of ketchup and brown sauce and the remaining table space is far too limited even for the least bulky of the Sunday red-tops. Not only that, I can guarantee that after having consumed this mountain of fat-filled bounty, I will always wish that I had done an extra egg and more beans so I can mop them up with the last couple of slices of bread. In my early running days I considered these greasy-spoon feasts as the perfect load-up for a demanding Sunday 'long one'. About an hour into such a run, my stomach decided to change my mind for ever. First it was the little crampo that came in waves and brought an extra, colder sweat to my brow, then came the stabbing pains a little lower down and finally the irrepressible need to defecate! Sixteen years on I would now like to publicly apologise to the members and friends of a certain squash club on the outskirts of Cambridge for the disgusting sight and smell that must have assaulted their senses every time they neared the main doorway to their preferred place of exercise! On this occasion I preferred not to assume the existence of a causal relationship between the toast and the turds but when events repeated themselves a week later (luckily in an area of secluded woodland), I reluctantly forswore the fry-ups in favour of some muesli or three, yes *three* (remember Ian Botham's fingers?) Shredded Wheat.

The pre-run meal is all-important in terms of content, quantity and also timing. We will look in a later chapter at pre-race routine, but running lore has it that you are better off not eating anything substantial within three hours of the start of your effort. I believe this to be way over the top and for most people half that time is sufficient for any excess to pass from palate to posterior and out. To run fast and well we need to be light and free of any feelings of bloat. Conversely we do not want to be hungry either and we must be sure that we have taken enough fuel on board to get us through the planned distance without any falling away of energy levels.

Back to those big breakfasts and their disadvantages. Not only are they disastrous scatologically speaking, but the high fat content does not provide us with ready sugars to burn and it can also provoke an overwhelming feeling of lethargy, sleepiness and unwillingness to push our limits. Sometimes even hours after a fried meal we still feel like the armchair and our bodies are one inseparable unit that only the imbibing of more caffeine-fortified hot beverages can pull apart. My move from frying pan to cereal bowl was not the complete solution. All cereals have a habit of aiding bowel movement and the absence of a solid (or at least non-liquid) visit to the toilet is dangerous indeed. From Frosties to Fruit 'n Fibre, breakfast cereals also tend to be very sugary and the normal procedure is to drown them in milk. Nothing wrong with that per se but more and more athletes are noting a degree of lactose intolerance which is reflected in an improvement in performance on the occasions when they abstain from the cow-juice for a day or two beforehand.

Another thing to bear in mind in the 'great athlete's breakfast debate' is the high **glycaemic index** (G.I.) of many cereals. The G.I. of a product is often listed on the packaging and is worth considering before any purchase of preferred foodstuffs. To simplify matters we can say that a product with a high G.I. will get its sugars into your bloodstream quickly whereas a low G.I. results in an often more beneficial, slow and regular release of glycogen. Opting for this lower end of the G.I. scale will do you the favour of helping you avoid any sudden crashes or surges in energy levels.

Many years of enjoyable experimentation at the breakfast table have led me to my current selection, which is a (normally huge) bowl of porridge, cooked with water only, on top of which I slap a very generous spoonful of marmalade. This combination ensures plenty of **carbs** and the medium to low **glycaemic index** of the oats provides a reassuringly long-lasting power supply for those longer sessions. To me it also tastes lovely and it gives me that warm, inner glow (aahh) that you see on the Ready Brek adverts. It never weighs heavily on my belly and even on those rare occasions that I venture out to race in an evening event, my usual super-sized helping of the Scottish Quaker's special with the obligatory quarter of a jar of Seville Thick-Cut sets me up a treat!

Needless to say (I'm saying it anyway), the importance of nutrition for athletes, if we road runners dare presume to call ourselves such, extends well beyond the few hours leading up to a run. We have already spoken of the general need to be relatively clean-living and to avoid too many dodgy stupefying substances. To what extent we emulate a teetotalling monk or nun is up to us. Even a weak lager can give a hangover, take the edge off our performance and start us on the slippery slope to a beer gut. On the other hand it would be fraudulent of me not to confess to the reader my discovery of the 'four-pint optimum', as it came to be known. Night-before-a-10k drinking became an enjoyable and welcome tradition as time after time the four large ones of Peroni or San Miguel incredibly seemed to push me to faster and faster times. Coincidence or not, I shall probably never know. However on one occasion my head throbbed for every inch of the way and I transferred my weekly allowance of alcohol back from Saturday to Friday evening.

Most of us have a pretty good understanding of what 'healthy eating' means. Stay out of McDonald's (unless you are burning it down, and even then it might be safer to work from the outside), grill don't fry, get your 'five a day' of fruit and veg, stay off the cream cakes, and so on and so forth. My friend Riccardo places particular importance on a hyper-healthy diet. He sits at his work desk munching carrots and refuses to economise when it comes to buying ingredients. What a supermarket calls *finest* he calls *basics*. For him training is as much about regulating what goes into your body as about what you can get out of it in your periods of physical exercise. For this reason he actually colour-codes the Excel spreadsheets that form his training diary. An easy-on-the-eye yellow or blue (this distinction depends on the number of kilometres covered) denotes an alcohol-free day on which his daily calorie-ration was not exceeded and he did not stoop to the depths of consuming an unhealthy snack. Brown, the colour of excrement, is reserved for the days when there is nothing temple-like about his treatment of his body. Riccardo loves to see expanses of yellow and blue as he scrolls back over his diary and this acts as a great motivator for him to stay on the righteous path. I should point out at this point that unlike many of the other human exemplars I have frog-marched into this narrative, Riccardo was more than happy to have his real name included. He even went as far as to suggest that I publish his contact details just in case there were any lonely female readers who fancied joining him on one of his brownest days!

What actually constitutes a truly healthy way of life and, more specifically, the ideal type of nutritional regime for us runners, is the subject of never-ending debate. Coaches argue constantly about the proportion of carbohydrates versus fats or protein that provides the optimum combination for the endurance athlete. Recently prominence has been given to scientific analysis that stresses the importance of not missing out on protein and quality fats. For those of you who prefer crunching numbers to crunching celery sticks, I don't think you can go far wrong if you try and get half your calories from **carbs**, principally in the form of pasta, rice, potatoes and other starchy foods. The remaining fifty percent can be split evenly between protein and fats. In practice if you eat good, fresh food and follow a Mediterranean-style diet, you should find yourself eating the right sort of balance of food-types without having to think about it.

The trouble is that here in cold 'Old Blighty', ever more influenced by shiny 'New Yankee', mamma and papà don't tend to spend half the morning picking the freshest fruit and vegetables and the rest of the day cooking them into something scrumptious. We are in the land of the crisp packet and the bargain bucket. *We* eat all the pies and *we* drink all the pints. Fast food makes fast money and as we perform our weekly supermarket sweep we cannot fail to notice that the sports nutrition sector must be raking it in as well. From being hidden away somewhere between the South American **quinoa** and the organic tofu, we now see that energy bars, drinks, powders and gels have gone emphatically mainstream. Seemingly in some kind of carefully marketed partnership with diet products, they now occupy their own aisle, but should we even consider spending our hard-earned cash on these garishly wrapped products that, in true Olympic spirit, shamelessly proclaim to make us go further, faster, stronger?

The major advantage of these energy products often lies in their convenience or user-friendliness. Far from cheap at a pound a pouch or more, energy gels can be slipped into the back pocket of a cycling jersey, carefully positioned in those inside pockets of your shorts supposedly designed for holding keys (but usually too small for that purpose), or even safety-pinned to the back of your vest. Grab as and when required, tear the top off with your teeth, squeeze, gulp and off you go, eighty-odd calories the richer and probably less than five minutes away from a noticeable surge of energy that will prolong your session or enable you to hold your pace to the finish line. I hate to admit it, but those little babies really do seem to work like magic. If only I had had them at my disposition some thirteen years ago as I neared the end of the cycling section of an **Ironman distance** triathlon. I had pedalled through the first hundred miles with the help of the energy drinks handed to me by the race marshals and with the added sustenance of a combination of dried figs and apricots that rapidly melted together into a sticky, congealed hybrid goo. Then, with twelve or so miles to go, came the dreaded **bonk**: legs went to jelly and it was all I could do to focus on the road ahead. Salvation eventually came in the form of half a packet's worth of glucose tablets which I crunched with gusto and washed down at the **transition** before heading out onto the marathon run. They worked a treat but I now know that a few well-timed shots of energy gel would have spared me my period of crisis. These days I always have at least one of my little 'gel-friends' to hand on any lengthy sporting outing.

Occasionally I will indulge in an energy bar too, but I am not a huge fan. They say that nature made its own energy bar and we called it a banana! The yellow fruit is indeed an energy-boosting snack and a lot cheaper than a bar. The trouble is that it doesn't take long for it to turn into a black fruit and it does not contain all the nutritionally engineered extra goodies (minerals, vitamins and so on) that the bars usually provide. Still, for me, bars are a largely unnecessary luxury. Wait till you get a couple as freebies after a race and then see if they make a genuine difference.

Treat energy drinks like you would hopefully treat the headlines of this Sunday's *News of the World*. That is to say, with a shovelful of scepticism. Frequently the side of the tub will instruct you to dilute the powder to a level which barely qualifies the resulting solution as a liquid. The sickly-sweet paste may well give you painful stomach spasms, that's if you can get it unstuck from the roof of your mouth. So if you want something more than good old H2O, just have some orange squash. Still not nutritionally advanced enough for you? Create your own recipe for the cheap alternative to commercially produced **isotonic** (big deal!) beverages. Dilute some orange juice, add some sugar or honey and a pinch of that aforementioned, cramp-preventing salt and Bob's not only your uncle but still in your pocket. A plethora of more inventive and doubtless better-tasting recipes can, of course, be found online. Whatever you may read, beetroot juice and extract of newt are *not* essential ingredients. If you really are too lazy to do anything other than take the 'scoop and shake' option, just make sure you end up with something more like squash than treacle, particularly on a hot day.

Those of you who have had the mixed blessing of spending a significant amount of time in the proximity of the noble equine will be familiar with the comical slopping sound that can emanate from a gelding's stomach as it trots or canters along after a few hefty slurps from the water-trough. A similar sloshing can be heard from the bellies of us runners too, if we overdo it on the liquids. Constantly we seem to have it drummed into us by the 'we know what's good for you', healthy-smiley, teeth-all-whitey media that we should be glugging down water all day long. The schools are full of kids repeatedly reaching for their bottles when they should be doing sums or reciting French verbs. No wonder that in the next lesson they are up and down to the toilets when they should be lighting Bunsen burners or checking their spellings. In the adult world the gymnasiums are infested with plonkers burning more calories in bringing their quick-release, calibrated, one-litre drinks bottles to their lips than in the paltry five minutes of running they puff their way through on the **treadmills**, which in turn are dominated by television screens blaring out MTV (telling us 'water *is* 'rock'n'roll'). I am not stupid enough to go against medical advice but a mixture of personal experience and anecdotal evidence has taught me that a moderate amount of fluid can get you through long runs and even longer rides without a problem. Marathon specialists complete the distance in under 2 hours 15 minutes on little more than a few sips and Riccardo (he of the brown diary-pages fame) regularly knocks out five- or six-hour cycle rides on no more than a couple of small bottles. Just make sure you are not dehydrated before you start. A good way of being sure is to check that you are passing clear, rather than yellow, urine. Don't be alarmed if a recent vitamin tablet has given you a hint of Dulux apple-green or if a forgotten glass of cranberry juice makes you panic at the thought that you are exsanguinating! After your run you will need to **hydrate**, after which you can perform the wee-wee check again to ensure you have done so successfully. During your run, unless you want to risk ending up doubled over with gut-cramps, diving for the bushes for a Paula Radcliffe-style bowel-evacuation or with an intestine sounding like waves lapping on the sand, **hydrate** but don't inundate.

As we turn our mind back to solid sports nutrition many of us will immediately think of pasta, a food that has been practically deified amongst endurance athletes. A few hundred grams of linguine al pesto and our glycogen levels are sorted, or so they would have us believe. Cyclists have even been seen breakfasting on the stuff! A Tour de France documentary showed a team of riders (not Italians, it has to be pointed out) tucking into a heap of tagliatelle topped not with your conventional ragù or carbonara sauce, but with marmalade!

At 350-odd calories in every hundred grams, pasta certainly packs in the **carbs**. From fettuccine to fusilli, or cannelloni to capelli d'angelo, the varieties are almost limitless and likewise, whether arrabbiata or alle vongole, the saucy combinations are irresistible. In days gone by I was a fanatical 'Pastafarian', so much so that when I used to race in Belgium, where they tend to favour an early afternoon start for their events, I would cram a couple of large, Tupperware lunchboxes full of penne al pomodoro for my pre- and post-race snacks! No wonder I would often feel uncomfortable a few kilometres into the races. Wonderful as it undoubtedly is, pasta does bloat you up! Admitting this to be true was a genuinely painful process for me, akin to rejecting my ancestry and betraying my forefathers! So much so that I still occasionally lapse into pre-race pasta mode and will often load up by eating an extra plateful of the stuff on the night before. Rice is the perfect alternative and for a shortish session a baked potato is a perfect, hypoallergenic choice. Depressingly unimaginative and English as it may be, it will usually keep you feeling slim and light and set you up nicely, as will the morning porridge I lauded earlier (add marmalade to taste).

We hear a lot about **carbo-loading** and about what to eat *before* we run but managing your post-exercise nutrition is equally crucial. After a long run, try to get something down you sharpish and don't ignore the protein element which may help to repair the muscle fibre damage that is necessarily incurred after an hour or more of giving your legs a drubbing. Commercially produced 'recovery drinks' tend to taste disgusting, although I have to admit that there is one 'rich-chocolate' flavoured variety that I am rather partial to. Don't forget either that all these concoctions are not exactly high on the list when it comes to the top one hundred diet foods as recommended by Weight Watchers, so go easy!

A fifteen-miler on a weekend morning tends to kick in, hunger-wise, later in the day. By mid-afternoon you will have succumbed to an attack of **the mungies** and headed for the cake tin or biscuit barrel, or both. If you have already made the mistake of ingesting nigh on a thousand calories of thick protein-packed recovery smoothies and an energy bar or two, it won't be long before you do the sums and work out that your big training day has actually caused you to put *on* weight rather than lose it.

A word of warning before we move on to the next chapter, which looks at how we can best get ourselves down to our ideal racing weight. We are runners, not jockeys (although one or two of you may be both) and we rely on *our* legs, not the horse's, being strong and staying strong. We need to be able to maintain our pace to the finish line without anyone whipping our flanks or kicking us repeatedly in the gut. Horses get their oats and so must we! They also get a sugar-lump or three if they are good. In these times of anorexia and bulimia we should never feel too guilty about an extra cup of tea or even a chocolate muffin, particularly if it helps to kick-start us into action.

MILE 13

MIRROR IN THE BATHROOM

This might not be pretty, so have a stiff drink, grit your teeth and brace yourself before you go for it. If things go to plan and you follow this chapter's advice, you will do it again in a few weeks' time and come away with an ego boost that will have you walking on air. We mentioned it in the goal-setting chapter, remember…?

Step one: Get naked! Step two: Stand in front of full-length mirror! Step three (once you have picked yourself up off the floor after fainting from the shock): Inhale deeply and breathe out slowly! Step four: Make sure nobody is watching you (no eyes peeping through the keyhole)! Step five: Jump up and down whilst observing carefully how much of your flesh is doing its own wobbly thing and not just moving skywards then floorwards in time with your jump! You should not have any trouble at all in retaining a clear and precise memory of this image. Like the most bone-chilling, hand-coming-out-of-the-ground, scary moment from a horror movie, the picture should haunt your mind for months after seeing it. Nevertheless, if your memory is a bit dodgy and you can be a hundred percent certain that your mobile will not fall into the wrong hands, you could dare to film yourself doing the bathroom jumps. I would guess that the last thing you would want is for this risqué, shocker of a scene to become a future YouTube classic. Keep the phone safe and when you return to the bathroom and the dreaded mirror, a month or so further down the line, having followed the forthcoming advice and put a decent period of consistent training under your belt, don't be afraid to film 'Naked Bathroom Jumping 2'! For once the sequel should be a lot more enjoyable than the original.

Back in the (nineteen) eighties there used to be a long-running television advert for a diet breakfast cereal. Along with 'Britain's Got Talent', the phrase 'diet breakfast cereal' must qualify as one of the most glaring oxymora of modern times. This annoying advert proclaimed, 'If you can pinch more than an inch, you need Special K!' The inch in question was brought to the viewers' attention as the all-teeth-and-hair mother in the perfect nuclear family squeezed the side of her perfect husband as he brought out the box of cereal to the perfectly laid table on the perfect lawn of a perfect house on a perfect summer's day. How many of us get to have breakfast in the garden with the sun already high in the sky? Any road up, *you* try pinching yourself just above the hip bone, on your side! If you can't manage to amass a good inch of chub between finger and thumb then you must have either lost your digits in a horrible workplace accident or your body-fat percentage must be in single figures and already at the levels displayed by elite Kenyan marathon runners. Needless to say, we can assume that the perceptive creators of the television commercial were well aware of this. All over Britain, people who previously considered themselves to be 'quite slim actually' were now self-certified porkers and were checking into liposuction clinics in their thousands. The reason for mentioning all this is that regularly pinching yourself in that region of your anatomy is a good way of monitoring the progress of your fat loss. Assuming that you don't have access to callipers or purpose-made electronic fat-content calculators, this is a far better method than just jumping on the notoriously inaccurate bathroom scales (especially those that purport to measure fat content), where the reading is affected by water retention, time of day, clothing, toilet habits and possibly even your eyesight! I have now joined my friends in becoming something of a compulsive pincher, not of female posteriors nor even of handbags, but of various parts of my own anatomy as I repeatedly monitor my inches! As I teasingly search for my six-pack or fondle my back to see if I am Special K-exempt, I want to feel rock not rubber, muscle not blubber, flat not fat.

Losing weight should be easy: you just have to burn more calories than you consume. Annoyingly for the food and drink aficionados that most of us are, our twenty-first-century, sedentary lifestyles don't require much more than one Mars bar, one sandwich and one pint of lager to provide our total daily energy requirement. The beauty of our sport is that, as we mentioned when we were looking at the idea of **running equivalent** training, we can add on a ton or more of calories for every mile that we run. Many food wrappers will optimistically tell you that the recommended daily calorie intake for women is 2,000 with the male of the species being permitted an extra 500. Stick to those figures and you will find it very hard to reduce the dimensions of your own figure. I know that to shed my love-handles I need to work on the basis of an allowance of 1850 calories per day to which I can add what I get through in my training. Let us imagine that on this average day of training I do an hour's cycle and a forty-minute run: that gives me, once I have checked my pace and done some elementary adding up, a total of about three thousand calories to munch through before turning in. My usual tactic, which is far from ideal, is to punish myself in the morning, going without in the first part of the day, and then to reward myself with a big bowl of pasta for dinner. I still slip under the duvet feeling hungry and this is as good an indicator as any that I am likely to be on the right side of the calories in versus calories out balance. If you give in to the grumbling in your tummy and have a pig-out before bed, it is possible to repair some of the damage with a morning run before you hit the breakfast cereal (but after you have been to the loo to get rid of the unwanted part of the previous night's excess).

'Breakfast like a king, lunch like a prince and dine like a pauper!' So they tell us, but the problem is that once you have had your 'full English' (vegetarian or otherwise), let it go down, and even forced yourself out for a run, the idea of getting through the rest of the day on a smoothie and some rice cakes is about as appealing and as daunting as doing a marathon backwards, dressed as a waiter and carrying a tray of topped-up champagne glasses. When you are calorie-counting and going to sleep feeling hungry every day of the week it can become psychologically oppressive and difficult to handle. I find that 'banking up' extra calories by exercising early in the day helps to take the pressure off. If you follow my 1850 calories a day starting point programme (to be adjusted up or down if you weigh a lot more or less than 75kg), I can pretty much guarantee that you will start to see pleasing results within ten days. By then your belt might get to the next hole and your pants might start to look unattractively saggy. Reward yourself with one day a week when you *are* allowed above your self-prescribed calorie limit. For this it makes sense to nominate the day when you tend to do the least training.

The other side of the coin is that you may well feel lethargic during your runs, you might get that light-headed feeling that tells you that you are lacking sugar, like when you stand up too quickly and it feels like your blood has abandoned your brain. Have a gel with you in case you really do have a sugar crisis. More often than not the symptoms will disappear and within minutes you will get a 'second wind' and wonder why you were starting to fear for your life. There will also be the odd Eureka moment when you have just got out of the car or the bath and it suddenly hits you that you have performed the movement with so much less effort than you used to. Use these moments to help motivate yourself to keep on track.

Hunger drives the wolf out of the wood. There will be days when the hole in your stomach that twists and nags *will* defeat you and take over your brain. Zombie-like you will be sucked towards the kitchen, like metal to a magnet. Be prepared for these occasions and try to pre-programme yourself to take avoiding action. If the situation occurs in the late evening it is particularly dangerous and you must try to divert yourself up the stairs and just go to bed. It's not easy to consume calories when you are asleep! Sleep is actually good for weight control because you will feel more relaxed and not be subject to the perilous cravings for caffeine and sugar that plague those of us who are not well rested. If you can't make the stairs then head for the tap and the fruit bowl. Try to fill yourself up on water and apples and with any luck you will fool your belly into thinking it has had its fill.

In the sidebar of every other website and on every other page of most magazines, the adverts for slimming products try to permeate our every waking moment, coaxing us with the promise of pounds being shed in the blink of an eye, 'or your money back!' There may well be tablets that speed up your metabolism and turn you into a rake in a matter of weeks. There may, though it seems unlikely, even be safe ones without side-effects. It may even be the case that Cho Yung tea will cause the rolls of fat to fall off you, but so what? You don't need these pills and potions and miracle remedies. You have willpower! The type of willpower that we are training here will carry over into your race and keep you going at race pace beyond the level of discomfort at which most mortals concede and start to walk. Just as we turn our back on steroids and other drugs that can directly, yet artificially, make us stronger or faster, so we should give the cold shoulder to the cheaters' tactics for losing weight. We want our success to be fully deserved, to be of our own making entirely and to be something that we can always be proud of, at whatever level. We want it to be achieved through hard effort, not the cowardly use of cash or credit card, don't we? Of course it is more than likely that all these concoctions *will* have come harmful after-effect. Don't give yourself the opportunity to find out!

As we have hinted already, it is vital that you don't leave yourself feeling too weak. You will soon learn to recognise the level of hunger that you can cope with and, perversely, you might even grow to enjoy the torment. Once you know you have the power to resist the food you don't really need and still retain enough energy to hammer through your next training session, then you can begin to smirk contentedly to yourself as your stomach grumbles and your gut gurgles away, recognising these as comforting audible reminders of your mission and your progress. Furthermore, you will gradually appreciate your food, its taste and its value, in a totally different and more intense way. There is a lot of truth in the dictum that 'hunger makes the best sauce'.

Even before you strip off and return, naked, to stand before that bathroom mirror, you may well begin to collect evidence of your evolutionary development towards *Homo speediens* having reached the next stage. At work people will occasionally do a double-take as they greet you with their customary 'good morning' or equivalent salutation, unsure what has changed about you. Unless you have shared with them your new-found determination to mutate into the slimmer, faster, stronger version of your former self, your colleagues are very unlikely to attribute your new slimline appearance to something born of your own deliberate efforts. Off-putting at first but then knowingly welcomed, typical follow-up comments to the morning acknowledgement include 'you look like I feel' and 'didn't you get any sleep last night?' Eventually these negative quasi-euphemisms will diminish in frequency and somebody will actually come out with what they meant to say in the first place: 'My God, you look thin!'

Then there are the visits to the houses of friends or relations that you have not seen for a while. Ageing aunts and mothers-in-law will gasp at the sight of you. 'Have you been ill?', 'Is my son (or daughter) not feeding you properly?' 'Are you stressed about something, dear?' You do your best to assure these over-concerned loved ones that even if there *were* to be a famine then you would still have several weeks' worth of fat deposits to draw energy from and to see you through, but it is usually to little or no avail. They now have a mission of their own, namely to feed you up again! With a verve that comes close to surpassing what you are putting into your training, they will bombard you with offers of roast dinners, doorstep sandwiches and triple scoops of luxury ice cream. If, after all that, they are still failing to lead you into temptation then they are wont to resort to the foolproof ploy of emotional blackmail. Out comes the perfectly risen Victoria sponge, at the centre of which an inch-thick layer of fresh cream and strawberry preserve protrudes enticingly over the sides. 'Look what I've made, especially for you! I know it's your favourite. You *always* have a nice big slice of sponge!' Can anybody stand their dietary ground in the face of a familial 'shock and awe' attack of this nature? At some point we all succumb (most of us are pushovers underneath) and make do with vowing to add twenty minutes on the end of our next run in a feeble attempt at obeisance to our calorie-controlled regime.

Don't expect the runner's diet to do wonders for your pulling power! As your Facebook profile picture shrinks with every update, those amongst you with 'relationship status: single' under your name will not necessarily see an inversely proportional growth in the attention you receive from the opposite sex (if that is where your preferences lie). As the girls gravitate towards size zero, their prize assets (particularly the upper body ones) may be sorely missed by their admirers. Whilst the boys might become more 'ripped', they are also likely to get less 'hench' and 'buff', which for many females may mean more turning off than turning on. What the heck does it matter? Soon you will only be concerned with the opinion of those who know how to appreciate the musculoskeletal elegance of the finely honed athlete.

Your metamorphosis into the runner that you wanted to be has now well and truly begun. Use that dreaded mirror to help you imagine the shape of the elite athlete you desire to see before you, emerging from your current contours. Become your own greatest fan and motivator. Assail your psyche with a barrage of positive self-talk of the following nature, banal as it may sound: 'Yes! You are doing it! You are becoming the best runner you can be! Keep it going! Don't give up! You are looking fitter every week!' and so on and so forth. Create a shining mental picture of *you the champion*, emanating light and a protective layer of positive energy, like a saint in a stained-glass window. You are on your way to the promised land.

MILE 14

GETTING STRONGER

Away from the eating and drinking, or more accurately the hunger and thirst, let's get back to the training. By now we have learnt that the self-evident agricultural truth 'no root – no fruit' is equally applicable to running. The root is the all-important base which we have now built (or at least know how to build) and now we have to look at what it is that we are actually cultivating and it is not a field of potatoes. We don't want to plod around forever like a sack of spuds, healthy and nutritious as they may be. We are growing succulent peaches on the tree of our potential Our aim is a plump and juicy crop of peak performances, back every year in ever greater numbers.

Our peach tree now has safe and solid roots, deep and far-reaching, sucking in the premium fuel of base training that we are providing them with on a daily basis. From this rootage there must now emerge the trunk: a trunk that will have to withstand the chill winds of tiredness, the hail of competition and even the lightning-strikes of injury. As we progress from root towards fruit, from fit runners towards fit and fast runners, we need to make sure that *our* trunk is strong. Strength in a distance runner is indispensable and it is not manifested in bulging biceps or sexy six-packs. It is a largely hidden, inner strength that matches that of the mind and is born of a special sort of training, a series of battles. Battles that will call for a toughening up of our core, the conquering of hills and learning never to quit.

Increasing our mileage and the cumulative effect of consistent running will take us some of the way, but potency and stamina should be maximised by introducing specific workouts that target our fortitude and tenacity. Ideally, these are brought in three months or so in advance of a peak performance and are made more demanding week on week before being reduced again to ensure freshness and to give way to speed-specific sessions as the race day approaches.

The fundamental principle behind strength training is that of increasing the load we put on our muscles so that they adapt to cope with it. Equally important is to keep the training specific to what we need as distance runners. We are not talking about a sustained programme of dead-lifting and bench-pressing the heaviest weights possible. The very fact that this is our chosen sport suggests that we are not of the endomorph body type that puts on muscle at the drop (or more accurately, the picking up) of a hat. If you do fall into this category you need to be careful, but most of us are mesomorphs (halfway houses) or ectomorphs (skinny, wimpy buggers) and the risk of an increase in muscle mass, and therefore in weight, that would offset the benefits of the training, is infinitesimal.

Short-distance specialists have led the way in this type of training and have not been short on imagination and ostentation. Increasing resistance to the running motion can be done by putting lead in your pants or a rucksack on your back, but to spread the load more evenly coaches have harnessed lorry tyres to their athletes and sent them down the home straight of the track! Even more dramatic is the sight of sprinters having a parachute opening up behind them as they battle ever harder to make it to the line. If you don't mind becoming the talk of your estate or village high street, feel free to adopt these extreme methods. You may wish to graduate upwards from a more modest starting point such as a motorbike tyre or a loose-fitting anorak that catches the wind.

Much more sensible is to make use of the best resistance training device in existence. It is provided free of charge by

Mother Nature and is called a hill. Even the flattest fenland dweller does not have to go far to find an incline that can be put to good use, for a mere flyover will suffice! Hill running is perfectly specific and will strengthen the very muscle combinations we need for our racing. It also hurts! Forcing yourself to complete the number of repetitions previously decided on will leave you rightly feeling like you have defeated an invisible enemy. As with all training, remember to progress gradually and one hard hill session a week is enough as your **quads** will need time to recover. Hill sessions can be done as **long reps, short reps** or even as a **fartlek** run and all are bound to help. If you need a template then try to find a hill that is not too steep to run fast on and that you can do at least fifty seconds of uphill running on. Start with four **reps** with a 'jog back down' recovery then build week on week by adding efforts or lengthening the uphill distance of each **rep**. Once you get to twelve or fourteen **reps** you could ease the mental and physical torture by splitting the session into two sets of six or seven with a longer recovery between the sets or you could alternate long and short efforts. The crucial thing is not to wimp out! Hill sessions are all about toughening you up and giving you an aggressive edge to your running which will translate into an ability to get the most out of yourself in a race. If you set out to run up your local 'beast' eight times and ramble home in shame after only six you are teaching yourself to give up. In the last mile of a race, as your opposite number makes a move, you will let them go instead of responding with the grit and lung-busting drive that could have taken you up to the summit of that slope for the seventh and eighth times.

At this stage there is little point in timing your efforts and looking for faster **splits** week on week. You may be starting the sessions with differing levels of tiredness and with a change in weather or ground conditions. As long as you run home or back to your car knowing that you have given your all then the training has to have been beneficial. During that final warm-down your legs should still be feeling heavy and a slow pace should seem like hard work. Nevertheless make sure you run that extra mile or two and do not go straight from hilltop to desktop. Ideally you will do some extensive stretching (bend your knee to bring the heel to your buttock to extend those **quads**) and have a hot bath or shower. If you really want that ice bath instead, go for it (you nutter)!

Running up and down the same hill often attracts the attention of the passer-by and a lack of self-consciousness and a sense of humour are essential tools in these situations. Comments like 'what's the weather like up there?', 'are you on a piece of elastic?' (actually that *would* be good for extra resistance) or 'you need better grip on those shoes mate 'cause you keep rolling back down again' are all too common. If they really start to get on your wick, a sharp, pointed 'why don't you join me … if you can?' usually shuts them up. Failing that you can always seek out a route that involves running a sequence of different hills. Go hard on every incline you meet and you have a ready-made hill **fartlek**.

Proper technique is overrated, as the essential thing is that you run in a way that feels right for you, but pumping your arms, keeping the stride length shortish and maintaining a straight posture should get you up the slope more efficiently and looking like a 'proper athlete' as you do so. Learning to run well when racing downhill is also a great secret weapon to possess. Tipping your head forward slightly should give the rest of your body an extra impetus to catch up with the weight of your head, almost like a controlled falling sensation. Keep relaxed, breathe regularly and deeply and try to make your contact with the ground more like a stone skimming the surface as it bounces across a flat lake than a pneumatic drill trying to break through the tarmac. To see how it should be done, watch a few videos of top fell runners, free of their flat caps and whippets, flying over hedges and stiles as they tear down Paddy's Pole or some other northern slope of torture.

In Italy I stay in a house on a country road. If I turn left I go up the mountain and if I turn right, yes, you've guessed it, I go down the mountain. For my first outing of the holiday I always turn left, heading up the steepening slopes, using the roadside markers to decide whether to go up that one more kilometre. More often than not I pass the odd ageing cyclist who either refuses to acknowledge my presence or comments vociferously yet breathlessly on how it is just not fair that I, with my two legs, should be overtaking him with his two wheels! On the way down the roles are dramatically reversed! Sweeping round the hairpins, freewheeling and gliding down like fearless falcons, the gleaming aluminium and Lycra disappears in the blink of an eye. Meanwhile I zigzag from one side of the road to the other, trying to maintain some form whilst not picking up so much momentum that avoiding a leap over the precipice at the next bend, propelled by the gradient, would involve sacrificing my nose and a few ribs against a fortuitously positioned tree-trunk. When the gradient gets wicked you can feel your **quads** taking a battering and your feet trying to force their way out of the ends of your trainers. I get back to the house feeling like I have conquered my surroundings and celebrate by consuming another mountain, this time one made of fresh Italian bread, pizzette and focaccia. I never learn! Year after year I defeat the mountain, consume the **carbs**, then, from the following morning onwards, I endure at least 72 hours of what feels like a dozen hammers beating at my thighs. The message here is that whatever you may feel, the hill is stronger and harder than you and, whether it's a flyover or Mont Blanc, it deserves respect. My old coach used to take his athletes, most of them middle-distance runners, to some local sand dunes. He devised a circuit and the idea was to take in about five of these little beauties, driving up each one as hard as we could. The biggest was probably less than twenty metres high but it wasn't long before we were tasting a mixture of blood and the grains of sand that we had kicked up into the dry air that we sucked in for all we were worth. The sand gives way as you stride into it and the extra effort needed to raise your knees encourages good form. After a sand dune session, Coach always ordered two days of very easy running.

Being a strong runner is more than just having strong legs. Sometimes top runners do look like a hybrid of the upper body of a small child and the legs of a horse, but the successful athletes that ignore their upper body and their core are few and far between. Even those minuscule Colombian Tour de France riders who break away on the steepest slopes and dance on their pedals like ballerinas spend many a winter hour doing press-ups, sit-ups and **dorsal raises**. As runners these are excellent exercises for us too. Stand at the finish line of any marathon and even amongst the fast boys and girls you will behold the give-away signs of a weak core. Hunched shoulders, an uneven gait, exaggerated hand movements and a rocking from side to side all betray a lack of conditioning. I recommend doing a set of press-ups to exhaustion (till you can't lift your body any more) at least twice a week and a combination of sit-ups and **dorsal raises** equally frequently. In these days of personal trainers, Swiss balls and myriad other toning and training aids, all promising to firm you up, you can vary your exercises all you like. I prefer to keep it simple and painful with the three exercises I have already mentioned. Every gym instructor will tell you that proper form is paramount and this is true. There is no point compromising technique to squeeze out your fiftieth press-up: that is competition against yourself and not what we are aiming for. Consult any training advisor, human, printed, online or otherwise to ensure you are doing things right.

Over the years we pick up little tips and variations on exercises that we feel are particularly useful to us as individuals with our own specific weaknesses. Many runners swear by lunges, while others sing the praises of the one-legged squat! Then there's 'the plough' and 'the plank', and best of all, the 'bird-dog exercise!' Kneel down and extend opposite legs and arms (not both pairs at the same time!). All these exercises improve the stability and posture we bring to our running. As soon as running form gives way our stride length tends to shorten and as a result we run slower. A favourite exercise of mine can actually be done as you run. If you feel yourself beginning to hunch over or you think your stride is shortening, run tall and bring your hands up so that your fingertips meet at the back of your head. Continue to run with your hands in this position for at least ten seconds. It may seem surprisingly difficult and it should allow you to feel any irregularities or imbalances in your running motion.

There are, if you look hard enough for them, dozens of ways to get yourself strong and 'fit to the core' available to you. From Jazzercise to boxing, medicine balls to mountain climbing, rowing to rock'n'roll dancing, as long as you are careful and recover properly, none of them will do you any harm. Don't let them replace your running, but don't ignore them either. Shocking your muscles by doing a new or different activity results in rapid adaptation and can be a quick fix for a lack of core fitness. I have a **'body circuit'** which dates back to my rowing days and involves sets of fifteen or twenty press-ups, squat thrusts, jumps, sit-ups, **burpees** and **wall-sits**. It takes less than ten minutes to do three sets but I am gasping by the end and secure in the knowledge that my fitness is coming back.

Combining a decent weekly mileage with regular strength training is physically and mentally demanding. To maintain this level of effort and to progress you have to be giving your running serious attention and importance and you will find that it is shaping you as a person. You may find, after weeks and months of looking at your watch during runs and counting repetitions, that your sense of time is extraordinarily accurate! I find myself being able to guess exactly how long I have been sitting dozing in an armchair, how many minutes it has taken me to write a letter, to wash up, and so on. You will probably also get into the habit of applying a hill session mentality to your work or household chores. 'I'll iron these five shirts, have a two-minute break, then iron five more.' You look at your speedometer as you are driving and find it easy to do the maths to work out exactly how long it will take you to reach your destination at your current speed. You get bored more easily and you find yourself constantly thinking ahead to your next hard run.

Once these symptoms have set in and you are training consistently and hard, the time has come. I hereby officially baptise you as a *proper athlete*! And what do proper athletes do? They race!

MILE 15

FIND A RACE!

Maybe the whole *raison d'être* of your running was a particular race: it could be the London Marathon or just a charity 5k that takes place in your area every year. Even if the latter describes your situation, this chapter on finding a race is for you and the reason is simple. You are unlikely to produce your peak performance in your first race, whether we are talking about your first ever or just the first of the season and therefore you should enter not one but several races. Top sportspeople are always telling us that they are 'coming into form', that they need a few more competitions to hit optimum, record-breaking form. Cyclists, sprinters, footballers, they all race or play themselves into champion shape, into peak condition. No runners want to go into the Olympics without a few testing contests behind them. They also all have *off* days. As we have mentioned before, if you put all your eggs in one basket, if you aim for one race and one race only, you are asking for trouble. There are factors which influence our health and mood on a particular day that are beyond our control. We cannot exist Howard Hughes-like, in total isolation, masked up against any possible passing viruses. Injury, ill-health, family strife and stress of all sorts can occur at any moment and to aim for one star run on one special day is a recipe for potential disappointment. The solution, as a distance runner, is to pick two or three build-up races, stepping stones to the big one. If on D-Day your race performance is more pear-shaped than a peach, at least you will have already enjoyed some of the fruit of your hard training in the preceding races.

Whatever your standard, never be daunted by entering a race. If you have followed the advice of this book so far, I guarantee that you will not come last (unless you somehow get yourself into the likes of an invitation-only 'Diamond League' track race). Even if you were to finish at the very back of the field, you would be compensated by getting the biggest cheer of the day, lots of new friends and the knowledge that 'the only way is up now'!

Finding a race has never been easier. As I write this I switch to internet mode and select one of the many sites, such as Runners' World, that list forthcoming events. On this midsummer weekend there are no fewer than 38 events to choose from, ranging from 5k to marathon, from road races to 'racing the train'!, from Cornwall to the Highlands of Scotland. This is just the list from one site. It does not include local fun runs, which can occasionally be better organised and more competitive than some of the so-called 'proper races' that come under the jurisdiction of UK Athletics or other bodies such as the Association of Running Clubs. Nor does the aforementioned figure of 37 include the ever-growing number of 'park runs', which are springing up all over the country. These are weekly 5k affairs which are run on Saturday mornings in parkland settings, as the name suggests. The other bonus is that they are free to enter, although you do have to register online and print off a barcode in advance.

The logical thing to do is to choose a low-key race as your starting point, preferably over a lesser distance than your eventual target race. Doing a mountain marathon as a warm-up for a flat **10k** would be somewhat counterproductive! It often helps psychologically to start the season by picking a run that takes place at a fair distance from your local area and therefore away from the gaze and interest of your rivals. This takes the pressure off and provides a benchmark which will give you confidence as you take on those you really want to beat. Evidently, if you are a novice runner this is less relevant, but it can still be nice to go somewhere new, where friends and family will be less willing to follow and you can focus entirely on your running and race day routine, of which much more in a later chapter. Make sure you visit the event website to assess the terrain and profile of the event. Do not go into a cross-country or fell race without the correct footwear or expecting to do anything like a best time for the specified distance. Look at the times of the winning athletes from previous runnings, then use a site like 'Powerof10' to see how they compare to their season's or personal bests. This will give a very good indication of how quick a course you are looking at. You can also look at how many runners usually take part and at comments made by competitors on the organisation, value for money, atmosphere and attractiveness of the route.

Maybe you don't want to commit to these subsidiary races too far in advance. You lead a busy life and have work, family or other commitments which can often result in a last-minute change of plan. If this is you then you may wish to pick a competition that has the option of runners entering on the day. This is usually a couple of quid dearer and there is the slight possibility of arriving to find the race full, but the organisers will usually warn of this if it is at all likely. Entering on the day allows you to wake up one Sunday morning, feeling good, and think to yourself 'I'm in the mood for racing'. Sometimes a race requires less mental fortitude than a training session as the adrenaline of competition performs the simultaneous magic act of motivation and pain-killing.

The mechanics of entering are probably simpler than making a purchase from Argos. As long as you know your date of birth, your address and your gender you should be alright! It has to be said that some runners' physiques, especially when combined with a gender-neutral coiffure, make the 'is it a he or a she?' debate a lively one for the more inquisitive individuals to be found in the pack. Don't forget to tick the 'M or F' box or you may find yourself being the first man to be called up for the ladies' first prize! This tends to happen if you have a name with an identical or very similar female or male equivalent (such as Francis/Frances). An entry form, on-line or on the day, asks you for your full name, your contact details and your club if you have one. Key in your card details or hand over the cash and that's it, you are *in*.

Entering a race that is not over a classic distance is another way of taking the pressure off. If you find a seven-mile race, for example, you will get a very good idea of your potential for a **10k**, without having the stress of having to live up to a previous best or being compared to the performances of your rivals or clubmates. You can follow up this kind of race by going into a standard distance event, ideally over a fast course, confident of matching or bettering the pace per mile you set in your preliminary effort.

Thousands of runners go into a marathon as racing virgins. These days the electronic chip will give them a genuine time but the size of the field and the nature of the course of most of the big marathons will combine to slow the opening pace to a shuffle until things thin out sufficiently for all runners to be able to move at their desired velocity. By doing a couple of smaller and shorter 'sharpeners', they would have accrued the self-belief to squeeze and push themselves nearer to the front at those mass-starts, which in turn would have meant a clearer course and a faster time. Small-scale events can still have atmosphere and are usually much better value for money. Best of all is the probability that you will be able to park within spitting distance of the start line and that you won't have to queue for twenty minutes for the loo. If you exceed expectations you shouldn't have to hang around too long for the prize giving and you can still be home for lunch!

The truth of the matter is (for how else would I have so many victories to my name?) that the standard of running in most distance races in the United Kingdom is pathetically low. I'm not moaning about this state of affairs, indeed it is great news for all of us athletes who are not *born* runners or the sons and daughters of former Olympic champions. It's great news because with a bit of *savoir faire* just about anybody who trains consistently and, *bien sûr*, follows the advice in this less than weighty tome, can have a realistic chance of winning an age category prize at the very least. 'But how?' you chorus. Well, welcome to the noble art of pot hunting!

Pot hunting for me used to be the practice of walking the back streets of south-east London in the hope of being offered some dodgy herbs to help enhance the street credentials of my friends from the suburbs who felt ill at ease in the ghetto that was 1980s Peckham. The pot we speak of here is not the sweet-scented sensimilla but the sweet reward for success in a race that is embodied in a trophy, shield or piece of glassware. Rewards that now clutter every spare shelf or sill in the homes of every triumphant athlete that has been fortunate enough to have heard the applause of his or her fellow runners as the prize, the beloved pot, is handed over.

Efficacious and lucrative pot hunting can be advantageous at all levels but it always depends on thorough scientific research, which in these days of instantly available information has never been easier. Even top Kenyans, some of the fastest runners in the world, are not beyond this fiendish skulduggery! Sure, they are not scouring the net for a race in an out of the way village that rewards the first three finishers in every five-year age category amongst a total field of less than fifty. *They* are looking for European races, within easy reach of an airport they can get to on a low-cost airline from the location of their previous race, that offer a decent financial incentive. Maybe the organisers can even be persuaded to cover travel, accommodation and entry costs. The stakes for them are higher than for us but the process and basic motivation is the same. It's all pot hunting!

La Chasse au Pot, as they don't call pot hunting in France, cannot be guaranteed to produce a podium moment. The point of any sort of hunting, be it for fox, moose or bear (as a vegetarian I don't advocate any of these), is that there is a challenge involved and an element of uncertainty to add excitement. Just as the fox can outwit or outspeed the hound, so as we become hound-like in our pursuit of our silverware prey, we can find ourselves thwarted by our own lack of rapidity or by a fellow hound in superior form on the day. Follow some basic guidelines, however, and it won't be long before you are pressing the flesh and collecting that first prize that will live in pride of place in your home and in your heart for many a year to come.

The first thing to ascertain is that there is indeed a pot to hunt! Many a time have I crossed the finish line, arms modestly raised to a little over nipple height, only to discover, as the last few vehicles exit the race car park, that the finishers' medal has been deemed by the organisers as sufficient reward for all. Fair enough, I suppose, but jolly annoying if that occasion happens to represent the pinnacle of your running career. Conversely, there have also been times when my name has been mispronounced through a crackling PA system and I have stepped forward to collect not only the customary shiny plastic cup or running figure but also a little envelope containing enough notes to cover my entry, my petrol money and at least one of the two new trainers I was after. So make sure there are prizes on offer and not just to the outright winners. Some events, as well as recognising veteran age groups, will give awards for five-year age groups all the way from 16 to 99! There might be lucrative team trophies and extras such as a cup for the first local resident, first unattached runner, oldest finisher and so on and so forth. If times are really dire you can resort to best fancy dress and if that fails too then try finishing last and going for the sympathy prize (often alcohol to slow you down even further).

Equally important in the pre-race handbook for pot hunters is the section on choosing the right distance and profile. Multi-terrain events over peculiar distances such as 8.9 miles tend to be a lot less keenly contested than an accurate ten-kilometre race on city-centre streets. Hilly courses, especially in the south of England, tend to keep the majority of the speed-merchants at bay. Consult previous years' results on the event website and assess the degree of talent present in relation to your capabilities. If the winners' names don't throw up reams of virtual pages of Google results then the likelihood is that the standard is not that high. Pick a race that suits your strengths and go for it.

Try racing out of season. Half-marathons and cross-country races are much easier to place well in during the summer months. These races are historically run in the spring/autumn and winter respectively. Not only that, the summer is when the most fleet-footed of the racing fraternity gravitate towards the track and knacker their **Achilles** tendons hammering those bends!

When you are in good shape, race often! That is the golden rule of the pot hunter. Maximise the prize-winning potential of your period of good form. Eventually things will come up trumps and you will get your grubby mits on one of those shiny things that you have always watched being handed over into somebody else's palm.

As you will have gathered, pot hunting is all about a kind of market research. Once you have assessed the most vulnerable areas or found a gap or niche that you are able to fill, you stride in and clean up. It's amazing what heights you can reach by using these methods. Big fish in small ponds tend to get a lot of recognition and as the rest of the world are not aware of the lack of competitiveness of certain areas of athletic competition, your achievements will sound very impressive to your average 'man on the Clapham omnibus'. The prime example of this can be found in the sports of **duathlon** and triathlon, although with their ever-increasing popularity things are not quite as easy as they used to be. If you are of a certain age and you pay your affiliation to the governing body, then as long as you can complete a race, no matter how slowly, you are practically guaranteed a place in the British team! How come? Well every year there are European and World Championships which are divided into five-year age groups. Because most countries do not cultivate age category racing as much as we do in the UK, each age group usually has a massive twenty places up for grabs! Given the cost of participation and travel you often find that the older age groups do not even get twenty people applying to fill them! So if you are a sixty year-old woman, buy yourself a bike, save up and train for a few months and 'hey presto' you will be an international athlete! Or so it was until very recently when British Triathlon introduced an extra criterion for some events which states that you must finish within 120 percent of the finishing time of the winner of your age group in your qualifying race. If we were to put this in marathon terms, let's say that the winner of your age group managed a time of three hours and twenty minutes, then all you would have to do to qualify would be to get under four hours. Again, by choosing a qualifying race in an out of the way location that does not normally attract the best of fields, it is clear that you don't exactly have to be an elite athlete to make the grade.

When you eventually get to the stage of relegating your trophies from pride of place in the living room cabinet to a pillow case in a dark corner of your attic, you have started to realise that although winning something is always fun, perpetual pot hunting can lose its attraction. What you want now are fast times! Back to the internet and the ranking tables for the various distances. Look for races with a concentration of fast times, where a majority of runners have recorded a personal or seasonal best. Seek out a fast, flat, city-centre course, guaranteed to be sheltered from the elements. Once you have found what you are looking for, enter early, as this kind of race can often fill up a month or more in advance.

We are all different and, psychologically speaking, we all have different reasons for wanting to race, for wanting to prove to ourselves and to others what we are capable of. For some runners the idea of racing is either too stressful or just seems to be in ideological opposition to the very reasons for which they run, reasons such as relaxation, stress relief, fitness, appreciation of their surroundings or even as a cheap way of commuting to work and back. Yet like Marmite, sex and the Channel tunnel, I believe everyone should try it, even if only once!

MILE 16

THE ICING ON THE CAKE

By this stage you are not just fit, you are strong and you are focused. You have got the necessary miles in your ever-skinnier legs and you have learnt the meaning of effort and tenacity by completing a series of strength-building sessions. What's more you have now entered at least one race. You are counting down the weeks, perhaps even the days, to that moment of fruition. In some respects you wish you could race right now, as the visualisation of the start line sends a stream of adrenaline around your body and into your brain. Most of the hard work is done. You know you can complete the distance and give a decent account of yourself. The cake is made, but it tastes so much better, and you go so much faster, with a layer of icing on top!

For me four or five 'icing' sessions are enough. I have a diesel engine with minimal capacity for turbo-charged acceleration. However much the engine is tuned, it's still a diesel and it performs better on long journeys than at Silverstone or Brands Hatch. The kind of **speedwork** that we will look at in this chapter might add five or six percent to my performance, but without thrashing myself on the track twice a week and risking injury. Others may have more in common with a Ferrari and will respond dramatically to the need for speed and the pedal being pushed down. If that is you, prepare to be amazed at how your fellow runners, the ones who left you gasping behind them on those long runs, are spluttering their way to the finish line a good ten seconds in arrears after each 400m repetition.

Since the last week before an important race, more if it's a marathon, is mostly about easing off and feeling fresh, it makes sense to start bringing the speedy stuff into your weekly routine about five weeks beforehand. These sessions are all about running much faster than your proposed race pace. They are about teaching your legs to turn over rapidly instead of chugging along at the rhythm you have instilled in them in all your steady miles. These sessions, like the **hill reps**, can leave you tasting blood and needing a day or two of pure recovery running afterwards.

The benefits, providing you don't overdo it, are manifold. Fast running will help you cope with those first few hundred yards of just about every race when it is almost impossible not to be sucked along by the pace of the fastest runners. The concertina effect dominoes through the whole field and everyone has to adjust their pace downwards as they check their watches and realise they are on course to give Mo Farah a run for his money. Short, sharp bursts of sprinting with brief **recovery periods** will teach your lungs and legs to cope with these fast starts and possibly also mid-race surges. I would never recommend these as a tactic to shake off the opposition, as it is tough to gauge how much they will take out of you later on. Moreover, you will be wanting to save that little something for the finish straight where you will be trying to outsprint your nearest competitor, hurtling to the tape to record a personal best, or just wanting to look good for your adoring fans!

The first session I will propose to you is a great way into the world of speed. As each effort only lasts twenty seconds it is not too daunting, and you can always look forward to the next bit of rest. Warm up thoroughly then do five lots of twenty seconds at about 95 percent effort, just short of a flat-out sprint, with just twenty seconds of slow jogging between each burst. The reward is then two whole minutes of easy running before you repeat the whole thing, take another easy two minutes, and do it all a third time. If at this final point you do not feel like your chest is about to explode it means that you have not been trying hard enough and your punishment is a fourth set of five times twenty seconds. That'll teach you! In many ways this session, given the brevity of the **recovery periods**, is as much a fitness session as it is **speedwork**. Nevertheless you will have done at least five minutes of seriously fast running and you will be buzzing for hours afterwards.

The shorter the efforts and the longer the **recovery period** between each one, the more we are working on pure speed. As race day beckons and we feel ready to race, we can give ourselves at least double the time of each repetition to recover, before we stride into the next one. As an example only, we might start a weekly run on grass involving ten lots of 300m five weeks before the race. The first couple of times we give ourselves a minute's rest. The third week we take a minute and a half. On the fourth we increase the rest to two minutes and in the last week we only do six efforts.

Help! I am starting to sound like a training manual and that is the antithesis of what this book and indeed running itself should be all about. Please ignore the detail if you want to. All I am trying to say boils down to little more than common sense. Our body adapts according to the training we have put it through. The endurance and strength work has been done and only needs to be maintained so as to not lose anything of the fitness we have gained. Adding extra miles in the last days and weeks risks leaving us with some residual tiredness during the actual race. What we *can* do is sharpen up and start to feel bouncier and lighter on our feet. As we reduce the long runs, however, and find ourselves spending less time hitting the road, it is unlikely that the curtailment of mileage will be matched by a proportional diminution in appetite! Take care not to set off all the gains you can make in this last phase of preparation by porking out on biscuits, chocolate cake and three bowls of pasta per meal. Now, more than ever, Lord, lead us not into temptation!

Ready to head out for your first proper speed workout? Think 'Location! Location!' Finding the right surface and surroundings is important. We need smooth, uninterrupted running during which we can focus on our pace and on maintaining proper form. Not possible if we are stepping up and down curbs or dodging traffic. The best option is usually to head for the grass of the local park or recreation ground, although these too can be a Pandora's box of session-subverting serpents! First there are the kids, the 'youff' with their obligatory hoods, fags and cheap alcohol. A passing runner is irresistible for those keen to show off their capacity for spur of the moment witticisms or, worse still, their capacity to run (for at least twenty metres) faster than you can. 'Run, Forest, Run!', 'Oi mate! London's that way!', 'You're gonna give yourself a heart attack!', 'Get those knees up!' – you have probably heard them all before. Then the hooded figure appears by your side, cigarette still lodged in corner of mouth, sprints a few yards ahead and then pulls over to the side, arms aloft, with a pseudo-victorious 'I beat ya! Easy!'. Easy to ignore, especially when you are, as you should be during this type of training, totally in *the zone*. Your eyes fixed straight ahead, you are determined that nothing will prevent you from completing the full workout at the desired intensity. Until, that is, you stumble headlong into the turf after tripping up on one of those kids' discarded cans or Bacardi Breezer bottles.

Even if you avoid the humiliation of the arse-over-tit scenario, the park session can be soured in several other ways. Failing daylight and the lack of artificial illumination can have you, in your heightened mental state of athletic endeavour, hallucinating veiled figures and gargantuan beasts emerging from the bushes. You find yourself veering wildly to the left or right and losing track of the timing of your effort. The twilight hours also hide the iniquities that can litter our otherwise green and pleasant parkland. Only on returning to the brightness of our front rooms do we become aware of the encrusted, stinking smear of dog excrement on our trainers or the remains of a hypodermic needle or used prophylactic.

Being in the zone deprives us of the usual social awareness and the customs that befit us as decent, gregarious human beings. If anyone should dare to ask us the time or for directions while we are in this trance-like yet dynamic state, the best they can expect is a derisory grunt. More likely is a spluttered expletive, a two-fingered salute, or a shower of saliva. Totally engrossed in our effort (paradoxically, rather like the day-dreaming driver who cannot remember the miles he or she has just covered), we lose conscious awareness of our surroundings. A line of naked beauties could stand in our path and we would just wave them angrily out of the way. Unfortunately I have never been able to put the truth of this conjecture to the test. What I have done is managed to offend many a dear neighbour who, days later, nervously asks me why I ignored them when I was running past. 'I didn't see you', though truthful, just doesn't wash. 'But I was standing in front of you, waving.' I try to explain: 'I didn't see you, honest! I was in the zone.' It still doesn't register as a remotely acceptable reason or justification and I have to think fast. 'Sorry, I was feeling stressed. Not myself. Hard day. Sorry. Can I buy you a drink?' That works.

There are infinite variations you can apply to the basic structure of a speed session. As long as your efforts are relatively short and you are exceeding race pace whilst running them, you will be producing something of the desired effect. Some athletes prefer to stick with unstructured **fartlek**, simply emphasising the shorter, faster bursts as they do so. Others swear by *pyramid* sessions where the length of each **rep** is greater than the preceding one till the halfway point of the workout (the peak of the pyramid) at which point the distances are staggered downwards again. A typical format might be a sequence of

200m-400m-600m-800m-600m-400m-200m with **recovery periods** rising through the session from one minute to two and back down again. If you are (sensibly) wary of the track, you can use the local football pitch: sprint across the diagonal then recover by jogging round two sides before striding out again.

'Icing the cake' sessions make you *feel* fast but you have to be careful not to overdo them to the point that your body assumes this new, super-fast pace as the preferred way to race. All too often we see 800m and 1500m track-running specialists delving into the unglamorous world of road racing and falling into the old trap of taking off at a much more rapid rate than they can hope to maintain for the whole **10k** or half-marathon. After two minutes' running they have a hundred-metre gap on everybody, but after two miles they are back in the pack, still naively driving their arms, their heads bent forward and shoulders hunched in the combined torment of lactic acid accumulation and fatigue. As you work through the final pre-race phase of your training, never lose awareness of what your actual race pace should be and how comfortable that feels, during the adrenaline-charged initial stages in particular. This is especially important for the longer race distances. If you fly through the first few miles of a marathon, even if convinced you are feeling fine, there is a long time left for you to pay. I know, and I have those photos of my tortured face to prove it. It is an excellent idea, therefore, to include a couple of key workouts in the two weeks before the race which are aimed at teaching your mind and body to know exactly what your desired 'minutes per mile' will feel like.

Now is the time to get your **Garmin** out (I told you earlier that they were only useful for measuring distances), but if you haven't got one ask your granny if she's got a trundle wheel tucked away in the attic or use your car if you are going to be running by the road. Failing these, just pace the distance out. For an adult with normal length thighs and shins, a big step is near enough equal to a metre. Perfect for this type of session is a stretch of 800 metres (approximately half a mile) or 1200 metres (three quarters of a mile) if you are feeling ultra-keen. Despite the unquestionable lowering of standards in the British education system, I would hope that most of us are capable of the basic mathematical calculation required to give us the time we should be taking for each 800m or 1200m, when travelling at the pace which would give us the marathon finishing time we would love to see on The Mall, The Champs-Élysées, or wherever our 42.195 kilometres will finally be complete. Feel free to discard the three decimal places, then divide away to get your target times. If you are desperate to get under three hours, for example, get your kilometre time by dividing 180 (the minutes) by 42.2 (the kilometres) then multiply by 0.8 or 1.2 to get the repetition time in minutes. A further multiplication will give you the time in seconds. **Answers** are in the back of the book! This is a race pace training workout and should not be too taxing. Your aim is to complete 8 **reps** of your chosen system *as close to target pace as possible*, it is *not* to try and complete the distance as quickly as possible! Give yourself a short **recovery period** of no more than one and a half minutes between each effort. Smile as you breeze through them and, crucially, imagine yourself at various points during the race. With any luck you will finish the last four furlongs feeling like you could do more. At this stage of proceedings, what's going on in your head is just as relevant as what's going on in your legs!

MILE 17

GO MENTAL

Assuming you want to pass, you don't prepare for an exam by forgetting all about it until the moment when the examiner tells you to turn the papers over and begin writing. Even if you know your stuff, you have to guard against being too confident or too nervous, you have to make sure you know which questions you are supposed to answer and you need to have an idea of the standard that is required of you. If, for example, the first question of your maths exam asks 'What is *Pi?*', and you spend the next two hours writing it down to two thousand decimal places, you may well be correct and have proven that your capacity for mental retention of figures is nigh-on superhuman. Nevertheless the chances are that you will fail your GCSE as you won't have time to answer the other forty-nine questions! It's like turning up for a race without having thought about what kind of effort is required. You run the first mile ahead of everybody, confident of victory, only to find yourself at the foot of a one-in-four climb that your legs give out on after just a few yards. The peloton comes streaming by, its members laughing or muttering a derisory 'unlucky, mate!'

To give yourself the best chance of passing an exam you don't just cover the whole syllabus, you analyse the exam format and the type of questions you are likely to be given and you make yourself aware of the time constraints. Best of all, you go through some past papers, perhaps even under test conditions. In the days leading up to it you think through answer after answer, making sure you have covered all the possible variations. Races are not exam papers and if this is your first race or the first time for the distance, you can't travel back in time to try out past editions. Doctor Who you are not. You do, however, have a tool that is your own little TARDIS. It can look forward, it can look back, it can play films in your head and it can rule your body, extracting from it feats you did not previously consider yourself capable of. Your *mind* might not move mountains but it *can* move your legs and *mental preparation*, as we already hinted in the 'Want it!' chapter, is a prerequisite to success.

Fun running, in its true sense of running *for fun*, has its own merits and if you really don't care about the outcome of your race in terms of time or position, then by all means just turn up and go for it with puerile naivety. You may well have lots of fun, but you are very unlikely to get anywhere near the levels you would have achieved by employing some tried and tested mental strategies.

We have mentioned how visualisation is crucial in those final race pace sessions but it is a tool that we can put to use in almost any waking moment and that can be beneficial from the first moment we consider the possibility of choosing a particular race right until when we actually cross the finish line. As we first read or hear about an event pictures spontaneously form in our minds. Maybe we can see the mass of club vests around us at the start, the long hill stretching menacingly up to the sky as we drive our arms to conquer it, or the clock at the finish line displaying a personal best. Try to turn every image into an instrument of positivity and encouragement. The club runners stand aside and nod appreciatively as you make your way, head held high and confident, looking lean and mean, to the front of the mass of nervous starters. The hill flattens out as you stride towards the crest, breathing strongly but evenly, still full of the energy that will take you to a glorious finish. We are starting to create a cerebral and subconscious association between the race and feelings of success and self-belief. As we gradually approach race day we must do all we can to intensify the connection and to make our mental imagery more complete, more accurate and more motivational.

Nothing beats an advance visit to the race route. Lance Armstrong would ride the crucial climbs of 'the Tour' time and time again in his training. For the time trials he would study every corner, every crack in the road. In my **duathlon** heyday I would travel to the other side of the country on the Wednesday before a race just to run and ride the course. A visit to the race location not only gives you the backdrop, but also the soundtrack and the atmosphere as you produce your pre-competition film. This is the three-dimensional movie that you must play over and over again in your mind in the lead-up to the big day. You are the star-protagonist and the producer. You have a co-director, however, and she goes by the name of Fate. Fate can fart in your face and lay you low with illness. She can conspire with the elements to deal you a race-day hand of thunder, lightning, wind and rain. She cannot be controlled, yet by accepting her creative contribution to your masterpiece the opportunities for her to betray you and the likelihood of her powers bringing you down can be minimised.

We gain this metaphysical superiority through common sense and by imagining and preparing for every foreseeable scenario. Our nous, our practicality, tells us to look after our health, avoiding excess stress and bacchanalian over-indulgence, accumulating good nights of slumber before the unavoidable pre-race insomnia. We are careful not to overdo the training, we decide on our race-day apparel and we make sure we are used to wearing it. More importantly, however, we get used to the race in our mind, well before we even pin on our number.

Our careful research, preferably supplemented by an anticipatory visit to the race location, has set the scene. On training runs, on the toilet, on the sofa, anywhere and everywhere, we fly from our actual surroundings and enter the fray. Our heartbeat quickens slightly as we hear the patter of trainers on tarmac, the shouts of encouragement from the few, reluctant family members that some self-important sod has dragged along to witness his ego-massaging endeavours. The heavy, increasingly strained breathing of the runners around us which we contrast with our own, regular respiration, even breaths that bear testimony to our ability to maintain this target pace which is too much for our competitors. In this version, perhaps destined for the cutting-room floor, the sun is shining and the air is still. Shorts and a racing singlet, we know the one that brings us luck, are sufficient protection. We enjoy the freedom of running with uncovered shoulders and knees, flowing freely past the one-, the two-, the three-kilometre markers. There is a runner just ahead, a pungent acidity, born of his sweat and toil, enters our nostrils, betraying his vulnerability. Always in control, always relaxed yet totally engrossed in our mission, we move alongside. Hills, wooded sections, the roar of a passing tractor, the screams of delight from the swings in the children's play area, the nine-kilometre point, they all come and go. No looking round, a surge of energy with the finish in reach, the left turn to the finish funnel and the final, give-it-everything push for the line. The after-race buzz, the knowing you have done all you could, the smiles and stories to swap with your fellow finishers, and the credits, credit to you (with the kind permission of Fate), to be continued…

Fear not, I have not lost myself totally in some warped runner's version of stream of consciousness surrealism. I am trying to bring to life the kind of visualisation that will bring you to the start line so well prepared that doing the race itself will be like visiting an old friend; a secure place that always brings happiness in the end. The film is constantly remade, the new version not supplanting, but providing an alternative to the last. This time there is the splash of puddles, the sensation of dampness reaching your feet through sodden socks which brings a smile, you knew it would come. The spray from the cars and the heels of the athlete just in front. A speck of mud enters your mouth and you feel its dirty grittiness on your teeth. Again you smile, it will not slow you down. The westerly wind, around the tight bend at the four-kilometre mark, is a smack in the face, but you were expecting it and the solid rhythm that carries you through towards the relative shelter of the line of poplars is like smacking it back. Others' heads are bowed but yours is held high and it shows on the finish line photograph, your mud-mottled lips elongated into a winner's smile, the smile of the conqueror of the race *and* of the elements. The hot bath on your return home, the satisfaction there to stay as the last of the soiled water disappears into the plughole. Each visualisation is different but always positive, always victorious, always fortifying an embryonic reality.

In the last days of preparation we study the five-day weather forecast and scour the websites and chat forums for the latest information. Normally we can get an idea of the approximate number of runners and maybe view the final entry list, where the more experienced amongst us will recognise the names that have topped the results list of other nearby races. Our visualisation can now include specific individuals and the comments we may have read may have helped us determine the pressure points or difficult aspects of the run. The starting area might be slippery, there could be a section where we are asked to run on the right hand side, new roadworks may have prompted a last-minute variation in the route. This kind of thing adds vital realism to our pre-race mental run-through. The verisimilitude of our preparation is enhanced further by focusing on how we are likely to feel and how we can adapt and cope with the unfortunate or unexpected elements without which every race would end up being perfect. Perhaps the most important aspect is with regard to the level of discomfort we are likely to experience. An optimum effort *will* hurt but with sufficiently vivid preparation we can teach ourselves to welcome the symptoms such as the shortness of breath, the strain on the thighs, the tightness in the gut (they vary for each one of us) and embrace them as the signs that all is going to plan. We need a very clear perception of the level of effort we know we will be able to tolerate so that at the start of the race we can reach it, rejoice in it and maintain it. Our mind's eye must extend to become also our mind's heart and lungs and legs. When we conjure up our race scenarios every sense must be active. As we add in possible twists of circumstance we make sure that we carry on and overcome them so as to still achieve our objectives. We see ourselves getting tripped over but we are straight back on our feet and driving on with added vigour; we get a stitch but we breathe out hard and stamp our feet to get rid of it and feel faster as we come through it. Our rivals surge ahead but we respond with controlled effort, gradually reeling them back in on the fishing hook we have attached to their collars. By the time race Sunday dawns we are ready for almost anything.

Naturally we have to be wary of over-stimulation. It is no good toeing the line feeling drained from our thousand and one mental rehearsals. We have to be mentally fresh. Worse still is a major case of that twenty-first-century syndrome which causes people to actually believe that if they really want something badly then it *can*, nay it *will* be theirs. So many people actually believe that bullshit! Maybe starving children just don't want food badly enough? It is no good being 'poor in condition, rich in ambition'.

Jill used to sell insurance and she believed it. She hadn't read much about running but she had read *How to Win Friends and Influence People* and various highly motivational company manuals. She loved paint-balling and team-building weekends. She did a parachute jump and a bungee jump and her sister dragged her along to watch her do a **10k**. Jill thought everyone looked very slow and decided she would give it a go the next year. She applied all her confidence-building techniques and even did a bit of training! She was so confident that she told everybody at work and at home and anyone else that would listen that she was going to beat her sister by at least five minutes and that she would probably win the whole race. She wanted it badly enough and she had visualised her moment of glory so well that nothing could go wrong. (After all, if you want it enough, you get it!) She bought the lightest trainers and the coolest sweat-wicking, skin-tight kit and, full of smiles, she weaved her way to the front. Right in the middle of the first row she smiled for the local paper's photographer and assumed a purposeful, arms-ready-to-pump starting position. She went on the B of the 'BANG!' and let herself be guided by her feeling of invincibility. Up with the leading men she smiled and she ran, unfazed by the increasing effort she was having to put in to hold her position. She was ready for the hill at the end of the first mile and she attacked it as planned. She knew not to give in to difficulties but to challenge them straight on. At the top of the hill she was still sharing the lead but her face was purple. The gradient reversed and she let her legs turn over quickly with the aid of gravity till, without any warning, her left thigh cramped up completely. In agony, she could just about manage a hobble. Her sister passed her two minutes later and she did the last four miles in a St John's Ambulance. She never raced again and maintains to this day that her misfortune was down to a mystery virus and that she could win a race any time, she just doesn't see the point! The point, the lesson you can learn from this, is that you should believe that you can perform better than in training and to the best of your ability but no, 'I *don't* believe I can fly!'

Studying how much improvement you can get from visualising properly is not an exact science and we should not factor it in as a percentage in our calculation of projected times. All I know for sure is that it helps and that most of us have not explored it to the full. Read about meditation techniques if you want to take it further and try things out. Try, for example, lying still and feeling each part of your body first tense and then relax. If you are still awake, try imagining yourself in a safe and warm place. Then picture yourself lit up by a bright light which warms you and makes you feel strong and totally safe. Now take that light with you as you play another version of the film of your upcoming race in the cinema of your brain. Try picturing yourself running just behind your favourite athlete, who covers the ground effortlessly and with perfect style. Gradually your own running comes to mirror that of the champion till, as you carry on running, with your bright light emanating from your body at every step, you merge into that athlete and then take their place. It is now *you* running gracefully and powerfully, attracting admiring glances from everyone you pass. Okay, like I said, don't be a 'Jill', don't get carried away! Hasty climbers have sudden falls!

MILE 18

RACE DAY ROUTINE

I get up a minimum of three hours before the gun, being careful not to crick my neck as I turn off the alarm clock, usually well before it was actually due to go off. Chances are I have slept very little and am already aware of the daylight streaking through the gap in the curtains. Going down my steep stairs I notice whether I am instinctively bringing my left foot to settle on the same step as the right before carrying on down to the next (an indication that my **Achilles** tendon is still sore), or swinging it youthfully through and down. I open the back door, breathe in the fresh air and stretch my hands to the sky. If it's dry I'll slip on some trainers, still semi-naked, and jog round the garden a few times, again gauging the freshness or otherwise of my legs. Next comes the shower and the temperature is dependent on how alert and 'up for it' I consider myself to be. If there is the slightest hint of lethargy in my body or depression in my mood I will force myself straight under the freezing-cold shower water, gritting my teeth until the warmer water gradually comes through, about thirty seconds later. When, on the other hand, my stomach is full of butterflies and my throat is dry with anticipation, then I will wait for the perfect level of water warmth before venturing under.

From the waist down I like to have my racing kit on, even before I start my journey. I may well put leggings over the top, but unless I am going to be racing in cross-country **spikes** I will always drive in my racing socks and shoes. I would go the whole way and have the top half ready to go as well, but the warm up and the nerves will make me sweaty and it feels good to put the racing vest and number on just before I head to the start line. It was not always thus, as I used to pride myself on minimising time away from home by arriving at a race seconds before the off! This usually meant that the drive to the venue would become something of a road rally affair. Racing technique was employed as red lights were ignored and fellow drivers were cut up left, right and centre. Anyone unfortunate enough to be travelling with me soon increased their range of vocabulary as expletive would follow expletive in English, Italian and the Caribbean patois learnt during my south-east London youth. Occasionally I would have to relinquish the wheel to my partner so that I could get my number on and be ready to go the second we arrived. I remember admitting defeat and heading for home after encountering heavy traffic on the way to a **duathlon** in Swindon, and there were two other occasions, both cross-country races, where my precision timing was not at its best.

The first, the Southern Cross Country Championships, was excusable since the venue was, as it still is now, Parliament Hill Fields in London. There was nowhere near enough to the start to park and in the end I was dropped off by my far-from-happy companion and had to clunk my way in my **spikes** across the tarmac and then over the grass to the base of the hill to join the massed ranks that I could just about make out. The trouble was that they were not getting any nearer. Indeed they were distancing themselves from me and were surging up the hill, jostling for position before the course narrowed. Unperturbed and full of adrenaline I gave chase with a fifty-second handicap and nine miles later finished the race in the kind of mid-table position I would have expected anyway! The second occurrence was that of the County Championships in the very un-London-like market town of March. No parking issues here and even the potato farmer in his big, red tractor could only hold me up for a few seconds before the straight, flat road was clear again, probably as far as Siberia. The reason for my lateness was fundamentally down to a state of indifference, a total lack of urgency, born perhaps of the multitude of mince pies and glasses of red that had been consumed throughout the Yuletide festivities. My determination and sporting single-mindedness, rather like the Christmas trees, had been discarded at the front door. Somewhere outside Chatteris (the wonderfully named band Half Man Half Biscuit, not locals, wrote a very disparaging song about that place) I knew I would miss the start. I carried on regardless, parked up and got changed and dawdled towards the start line, not expecting to do anything other than spectate, only to find myself being shouted at by a county official. 'Off you go,' he barked,' we'll time you separately!' So off I went, eventually catching the rear of the field and passing runners at ever more frequent intervals for the rest of the race. I finished outside the top ten but in a good time and shortly afterwards received a letter stating that I had been successful in gaining selection for the county team and asking me to represent Cambridgeshire at the 'Inter-Counties' in late January. I was not late for that!

Back to the race day routine, and if you remember I had just got dressed. Next I head for the porridge box and pour a generous helping into the saucepan. As mentioned in a previous chapter, I cook it with boiling water, only because the anecdotal evidence for the consumption of large amounts of dairy product on race day adversely affecting performance is pretty sizeable. I make up for the blandness of the porridge with the quarter of a jar of marmalade I bung on top. Exact quantities will depend on the length of the race ahead but I don't hold back! A final check of the kit bag for all the essential items (remainder of racing kit, pins, gels, Vaseline, towel, post-race clothing, money) is followed by a final visit to the lavatory. A successful evacuation of the bowels, as we already know, is a good indicator of being in the right state of heightened anticipation for the race. Better out than in. The lighter we are the better.

In the car I will regularly sip orange squash or an energy drink to ensure not only proper hydration but also that I will be busting for a pee by the time I get to the event headquarters. Rarely do I make it to the designated toilets with their obligatory queue of anxious runners who are trying to make their hopping from foot to foot, evidently provoked by a hyper-inflated bladder, look like some kind of sophisticated warm-up. Usually a tree near the car park gets the benefit of my effluence, although in certain surroundings I have had to engage in some intricate hand-eye co-ordination, sandwiched between the open front and back doors of the car for modesty, in order to keep shoes, legs and car upholstery safe from the urinary trajectory.

Dietary planning for a race begins well before the day of competition. A high carbohydrate diet and an avoidance of toxins will see us through the shorter distances, even if we are blessed with the speediest of metabolisms. Once we get to half-marathon and above we can enjoy some guilt-free **carbo-loading**. This might just mean an extra spoonful of rice or forkful of pasta, or maybe a slice of cake and a bottle of energy drink on the side as we try to relax on the evening before the big day. Serious carbo-loaders, however, begin a *week* before by depleting their glycogen stores. If the race is on a Sunday then from the Saturday eight days beforehand until the Tuesday or Wednesday of race week, Mr Carbo Loda himself will deliberately avoid all starchy foods and augment the protein component of his diet. Carbo will feel sluggish and light-headed in his training. When he stands up quickly he will feel like he is going to faint and he welcomes this feeling! He welcomes it because it is nearly Wednesday evening and the start of a glorious eighty hours of no-holding-back rice and pasta fest! In the days before the race he feels the energy levels increase each morning. The body is scared of being depleted again and so is sucking in and retaining every ounce of fuel it can, as if preparing for a famine. Training sessions are brief, with the odd bit of

speedwork to keep him feeling spicy. By Saturday evening he is not sure if he can look another bowl of spaghetti in the eye and he is starting to feel bloated. Race morning nerves take care of that! Our bodies can only store a limited amount of available glycogen and by the twenty-third mile of his marathon even Mr Loda will be grateful for his sachet of energy gel. He is still running strong, however, unlike his compatriot and namesake, Mr Carbo Ignora.

Each of us responds differently to nutritional experimentation of this sort and it is definitely worth trialling the procedure before putting it into practice for an important race. What is vital is that we don't under-eat before a long race. Hand in hand with the pre-race carbohydrate consumption goes the pre-race **taper**. We want our legs feeling fresh and bouncy when we get there, even if it's after a long drive.

A reformed character, I now tend to show up at least 45 minutes before gun-time. This allows an unhurried period for number collection if necessary and for the unavoidable chats with fellow athletes falling over each other to bombard me with their myriad excuses for the poor performance which they say is bound to follow but only very rarely does. Thirty minutes to the start and it's time for the warm-up, namely a slow run of eight to ten minutes followed by some stretching and then some relaxed strides. Doing these in front of the amassed opposition right by the start line will make many lesser runners feel like going home, while others will be all the more determined to beat you. Typical behaviour for the world-class, elite athlete is to warm up alone, a time for sampling the ground and weather conditions and for a final run through of that mental film of the race to come. Fifteen minutes to go and I gulp down an energy gel, another piece of physical and psychological insurance against running out of steam. I get my vest and number on and make sure I have time to get to the front of the pack before the start time. Once I am there it is as if an external force takes over. The film has started rolling and it will carry me along. Everything has a predetermined quality. Nerves disappear and a confident smile spreads across my face.

There is nothing special about my race day routine and I have described it more to illustrate my quirky amateurishness than to recommend its efficacy. The key thing here is that the routine exists and now acts as an almost guaranteed precursor to a pleasing performance. By definition a routine cannot exist until it has been repeated, so if you do not have one already in place, create a template, a written checklist or a carefully memorised sequence, a strategy that can be adapted and refined with every subsequent execution. Bemusing as it might be for your co-habitants, I would suggest a dry run, three or four days before the one that counts. Give yourself more time than you would normally allow for the everyday things like brushing your teeth or having a shave! The chances are that your mind will wander back into that race-route movie and five or so minutes will be lost in a trance-like torpor before you come round, suddenly aware that you are chewing your toothbrush or carving a hole into your cheek with your razor.

You may well experience waves of extreme nervousness or nausea as you count down the hours and then the minutes. At these times just take a deep breath and smile and tell yourself that this is not life or death, nor is it 'more important than that', as Bill Shankly once said about football. Remind yourself that you had a choice, that nobody forced you to do it, and you chose to do it to make yourself feel good, not to feel sick like this. Bring to your mind that in a matter of less than the length of a working day, it will all be over and you will have moved on, with other pressing matters to occupy your mind. If, on the other hand, you are feeling sluggish and uninspired, give yourself a good hard slap around the face, try the cold shower treatment and stick on some upbeat tunes, nice and loud. Still not up for it? Threaten yourself with self-torture and then start to carry it out. Once you start feeling the pain of your testicles being crushed, the idea of a good hard race will seem uncommonly appealing!

The athlete that is going to succeed knows how to achieve the correct level of arousal before a race. He or she will not be affected negatively by an unexpected event, such as the start time being put back or adverse weather conditions. Make sure *you* have the confidence to handle such things and stay positive throughout your warm-up. Stay away from people who you know will want to beat you or those that want to let you know that they are not in top shape, so that if they do in fact finish ahead of you it will be like a double blow. You have worked hard for this and need to do yourself justice, something that will come from within. A complete athlete should not need their coach or any support team in the minutes before a race sets off. Use these valuable moments to visualise the start and finish, ideally actually running those first and last hundred yards, imagining yourself staying calm and flowing easily for the former and giving absolutely everything in the latter.

I bounce up and down and hear the starter thank the marshals and warn us of the possible hazards of which my pre-race preparation has already made me aware. I sense that other runners are aware of my confidence and I draw further strength from this. From time to time runners will devote their last words, before their breath is taken by the starting gun and then by the effort of racing, to psychological sparring. 'You should win this one!' 'Yeah, easy!' is my retort and I don't make eye contact. I put my right foot forward to the line and: 'Attention! Set! Go!'

MILE 19

RACING CLEVER

Some people just don't want to do well, it seems. Regardless of their level of fitness, they race like total plonkers. I've given up politely pointing the odd thing out to them as they always repeat their mistakes. It's like the cyclist who rides a race in an anorak that flaps in the wind, on a bike with a chain that is caked in gunk and wheels with under-inflated tyres. He's trained for six months to get ten seconds a mile quicker and now he loses double that by just being too lazy or ignorant to wear something tighter, clean his bike and use a pump. Plonker!

Maybe the runner can't afford a lighter pair of trainers – fair enough! Maybe there are medical reasons for needing the extra cushioning and the compression socks. Unlikely, but fair enough! Maybe he has a particular hypersensitivity to the cold and feels like he runs better in his long-sleeved track-suit top. Very unlikely, but fair enough! There are *no* excuses for headphones (they are a menace), *no* excuses for carrying a bunch of keys (just hide them somewhere if nobody will look after them), and *no* excuses for carrying a water bottle, or worse still one of those poxy Camelbaks (rucksacks in disguise) when there are regular water stations anyway. Maybe the plonker is just running for fun but he should get out of the way of those of us who are racing!

Distance running is not the place for complex racing tactics. Psychologists and physiologists agree that the best times will come from even paced running. To achieve your best time, *all other things being equal,* you should run at the maximum effort that you can hold for the full required distance. Your race pace has to feel if not comfortable, then at least familiar. We all have different thresholds and different reasons for not being able to go that fraction harder. Some of us complain of our legs giving out, others can't hold good form and, for most of us, we just can't get the oxygen to our muscles fast enough, we get out of breath and it bloomin' hurts! It's all about finding the ideal pace, settling into it and enjoying it. This is where those race-pace repetition sessions come into their own. Think back to them, remember how they felt, how your legs were turning over, and try to replicate it! The likelihood is that the buzz of racing will give you an extra gear that you will not be aware of and you will go through the first mile in well under your projected time. Congratulate yourself on this, tell yourself what a good race you are having, but don't get carried away.

As you run, monitor your wind! I am not asking you to conduct a chemical analysis of your burps and farts here, but to assess the intensity of your effort by the rate and depth of your breathing. Now comes the million-pound question (you can't ask the audience, phone a friend or go fifty-fifty), and you have to keep asking it throughout the race. Can you hold your current pace for the whole of the distance that is left? Often the honest answer will be 'not quite' and this is when it takes a strange type of courage to actually ease off a touch. Don't be humbled by the fact that those around you seem to be trying harder and yet are not choosing to slow down. Just because they sound like baboons giving birth, it doesn't mean that your comparatively silent striving is any less whole-hearted or 'whole-lung'd'. *You* know your limits and you must respect them. Getting to the five-mile marker two minutes ahead of schedule will not make for a pleasant finish to your half-marathon. Apologies for the repetition, but this is crucial stuff. Always be aware of how long you have to go and ask the question again and again. 'Can I keep this pace up?' Don't be afraid of feeling like it's too easy; I can count on the blisters of one un-Vaselined heel the number of times I have known anyone who has prepared properly for a race and internalised the nature of the course actually finish the race believing that they should have gone harder in the early stages. It only takes a glance at the watch or at the rhythm of the athletes ahead to give us a pretty accurate idea of where we are compared to our target pace. If we make a mental miscalculation or overestimate the intensity of our running and get to half way significantly later than we intended, it is still not time to panic. We still have a powerful piece of magic tucked up our shorts (we haven't got any sleeves to keep it up), and it's called the **negative split**!

On several occasions I have been employed by my friends, unfortunately without any financial recompense, as a pacemaker. No, I am not a human beta-blocking heart monitor, but somebody who has learnt from years of quotidian running what travelling at various speeds feels like. 'I reckon this is 6.15 miling,' says Jim. 'More like 6.22,' I might reply, and I am usually right. If I am sitting in a room without a watch on or a clock to look at, I can often guess the time before checking it with almost frightening accuracy. What a talent, eh? Getting back to the pacemaking, the idea of it is to drag my ambitious companion to a new best. Sadly, though my pacemaking might be spot on, the aspirations of my followers are often not and their over-ambition becomes more than apparent after just a couple of miles when they start to see me weaving from side to side to give them time to catch up. The truth hits hard and they don't want me there rubbing it in. 'Go on at your own pace!' they cry, in a mixture of anger, altruism and martyrdom. I don't need telling twice and off I go, revelling in the 'coming from behind' scenario as I overtake runner after runner. The crazy thing is that on two or three occasions I have come very close to achieving record times in this manner. It really is the case that a race *can* be rescued and turned into victory after a (comparatively speaking) very slow start. Running a **negative split** has come to mean running the second half of a race faster than the first and of course it is in theory harder than maintaining even pace all the way. In the circumstances I have outlined, the **negative split** was drastic and still came good. If you get to halfway only marginally down on your predictions and the reason is that you have made sure that you have stayed at a manageable pace, then you have every reason to be confident still. Grit your teeth and go for it! Many people are forced into **negative split** situations in mass-participation marathons where the congestion in the early miles puts a lid on their over-eagerness to chew up the miles, and often it is a blessing in disguise.

Falling behind schedule can just result from getting your times mixed up. If numbers and memory don't go together in your poor little brain, you can always write them (in *permanent* ink) on the back of your hand. This is also a great place to write your favourite mantra that you know will help you during the race, as well as in training, when you need it. You can go for 'stay relaxed', 'you are a winner', 'never give up' or you can actually be original and imaginative. My favourite is 'If you can read this, you are not trying hard enough!'

Of course there is a lot more to racing well than just finding the correct cruising speed, although you can get a heck of a long way on that alone. Occasionally things outside of your control will seemingly conspire against you and you need to know how to react. Foremost amongst these is the evil arch-enemy of the personal best who goes by the name of 'headwind'. When he comes out to play you need to hide. Look for shelter by keeping in close to a wall or a line of trees! Better still, make an extra push to get yourself tucked in behind the runner up ahead (with any luck he will be seven foot tall and broad-shouldered). Once you are there, nicely shielded from the gale-force destroyer, he will be making twice the effort that you are and you can bide your time till a change of direction strips him of his purpose and you can discard him like a lover who has lost all novelty value!

The chances are that he will not have enough energy left to repay the compliment and use you in the same way. Top of the list of windbreakers, however, is the lead vehicle: if you know you are going to be up at the sharp end it is well worth slipping the driver a fiver to get him to stay nice and close during those headwind sections. If that goes against your sense of fair play you can just hope that the driver is naive enough to be unaware of the drafting effect he is providing for you.

Even though as runners we are all aiming for the same personal victories, we are also competitors and some of us are prepared to go further than others to get that winning edge. At the dirty end of the scale is the not so accidental clipping of the heels or the nudge with the elbow. The 'cutting up' that makes us brake and lose our tempo like cyclists who see the car that has overtaken them suddenly turning left across their path. Most off-putting of all is the spitting to the side that results in the globules of saliva being carried on the breeze into our faces. My advice here is to wipe it off and smear it back over the spitter's T-shirt as you overtake! Be prepared for these things and laugh inwardly at them, for they are usually signs of weakness.

Bluffing is less common in running than in poker, cycling or double-glazing sales, but it does exist and I freely admit to being guilty of it. From the false modesty of the self-deprecating comments at the start line to the simulated mouth-closed, relaxed look for the photographer at the finish. During the race itself, there are times when it pays to make yourself look exaggeratedly good, but also when it can be of use to fake extreme suffering. Remember that seven-footer we were hiding behind to cheat the wind? What if he turns round and says, 'Come on, you come to the front and do your share!' Assuming you are not in the mood for a post-race punch-up with someone twice your size, this is the time to earn your running Oscar. As if unable to conjure up enough spare breath to utter actual words, spread your arms slightly in a gesture of helplessness, go cross-eyed with apparent exhaustion and, tongue lolling at the side of your mouth, let out a meaningless grunt that bears a vague resemblance to the words, 'I can't'. As you fly past after the next bend in the road, try to sound genuinely like you want to repay the favour as you say, 'Okay, you tuck in now!' Next race, you may well want to find a different giant to hide behind.

Demoralising your rivals by looking excessively comfortable or pretending to strike up a conversation is largely counter-productive and faking superiority is of limited value. If, however, you are racing alongside someone who you know has the beating of you in an out and out sprint to the finish line, you may need to find a way of breaking them psychologically. It is when results in terms of finishing position are more important than finishing times that tactics can really come in useful. Hopefully you trained to reduce your weaknesses but now is the time to race to your strengths. If you have the ability to cope with changes in pace you have a lethal tool in your weaponry. It is incredible how just a couple of surges can punch out the self-belief of a pursuer. If you can handle surges, wait for a bend when you can get momentarily out of sight of the runner on your tail and stick in ten fast strides. On rounding the corner the following runners will believe that they are fading or that you are super-strong and may give up the fight there and then. It never ceases to amaze me how a tiny increase in pace can have a devastating effect. On the occasions where I have put this tactic to good use, a backward glance, saved for well after the faster stretch has ended so as to not betray the degree of exertion, has always revealed a race-defining gap.

Maybe *you* are the girl or guy with the blistering final sprint. You have to remember the knicker-elastic that connects you to your quarry in front. Never let it get too stretched. Have total faith in yourself and respond to every move, reminding yourself that what hurts you hurts the other runner just as much. You know you have that sixth gear that will win you the race if you can just hang in there. Never let that elastic snap! You don't want to finish with your drawers round your ankles!

Even with the most meticulous preparation possible and the greatest attention to every detail, another thing that you cannot guarantee is your underlying mood during a race. Feeling great from start to finish doesn't often happen, unfortunately, and just as we prepare for the hills and the wind, we have to know how to cope with those moments or longer periods when the going gets tough and our mind wants to instruct our legs to slow down. You can make sure you get out of bed on the right side and wear your lucky pants (though it's more hygienic to go without), you can batter your brain with positive self-talk and motivating mantras, you can force your face to smile, yet still you will be vulnerable to what is after all the logical consequence of our mind acting as protector and guardian of our body: namely the desire (which can soon metamorphose into a craving and then a physical need) to *just slow down*. Don't just hope the feeling will go away! It might, but by then it could be too late to rescue your performance. Accept the tough times and use them as a spur to take a different mental approach to the race. Usually, in these moments of athletic anguish, we are daunted by the distance and time that we still have to run. Admit to yourself that there is a long way to go but convince yourself that you are strong enough at least to get to the next bend, the next distance marker, or just to the next lamppost or tree. As you approach this first target, persuade yourself that you have got what it takes to get to the next one, and the next. You may well find that it soon becomes easier to hit the next target and by drawing confidence from each section you complete you can inspire your mind and fool your body into feeling fresher and faster. This 'segmentation' of the distance is a tried and tested technique amongst marathon runners but do not rely on it or use it too early on. The rational mind will soon win out if you are already pushing from telegraph pole to lamppost with twenty-three miles still to cover. Your training has made your legs solid, sinewy and resistant to pain and the same should be true of your mind. When times are hard and you feel like the race is slipping away from you, think back to those endless training runs and the gut-busting, lung-rasping, uphill repetitions. 'They hurt me more than this can', tell yourself, and make sure you win the mental and the physical battle at the same time. Defeat is not an option.

Often we can find ourselves in the situation where our watch is telling us that things are going to be very close. Maybe we are on course for beating our previous best but only by a few seconds and we know that the last mile is slightly uphill. Alternatively, our rivals could be running beside us, matching us stride for stride, and we just can't seem to shake them off. Faced with this kind of problem, the first thing to do is to congratulate yourself on what you have already accomplished. Reminding yourself that the very fact of being in this situation is already a significant achievement will help you stay calm. Next you need a strategy that will give you that fraction extra that will make your race a complete success. Many athletes will try to 'attack' on uphill sections and you need to anticipate this, driving hard and sticking like glue to the shoulder of your adversary. If you reach the top of the incline together, *now* is the time to put in a surge. Runners don't expect an acceleration when the road heads downhill and, already out of breath from the preceding climb, they may well be far from keen to respond. If you are on your own, going for a time, again use the downward slopes to gain a few seconds. You can also use mile or kilometre markers as starting points for ten or twenty seconds of effort before returning to your previous pace. When the finish clock appears, those tiny savings should have added up to make all the difference.

Time to stop sounding like a 'born-again' evangelist. I'm not trying to convince you that by believing you will be saved, that by visualisation you will smash your **PB**, or that with properly thought out tactics you can run the legs off a competitor half your size and twenty years your younger. I *am* saying that *without* belief, visualisation and sound tactics you are jeopardising your chances of achieving what your improvements in fitness have made you capable of.

This next bit of advice, if you don't already follow it, will shave more off your race times than years of training. It costs nothing and requires no effort other than keeping your eyes open! When I race on the road and even on the country I am amazed at how so many athletes, including some very fleet-footed ones, still don't do this. Why do so many runners follow the course as if they are attached to some rail-line or overhead tram wire? Do they think they are still on the track running 200 metres and that they will be disqualified if they put one foot outside of their lane? In cross country races you don't have to hug the perimeter of fields or wooded areas as long as you stay the correct side of what markers there are. As a road runner there is no rule that tells you that you have to stay six inches away from the left hand curb at all times. When the old boy from UK Athletics comes out to measure your course on his 'old faithful' bike with its perfectly calibrated measuring wheel, he will not be setting out to do you any favours to help you make the course short and fast. He takes a sneaky pride in every foot he can shave off and that in turn you will have to add on if you don't follow his line.

The course measurer is under strict instructions to take the shortest available, permitted track at all times. Your aim should be to make it even shorter as you run the race. If you have been told to keep to the left, do so, but allow yourself to go out as far as the centre of the road (being careful, of course) when that is the advantageous thing to do. ALWAYS AIM TO TAKE THE SHORTEST LINE BETWEEN WHERE YOU ARE AND THE FURTHEST POINT ON THE COURSE THAT YOU CAN SEE! I pride myself on my ability to do this and am certain that I owe several of my victories, at least in part, to this technique. Nobody out-shortcuts me! I have been known to jump over walls, run through people's front gardens, push spectators out of the way and splash through knee-high puddles. I also regularly grab hold of marshals so as to spin round them quicker when they are standing still to mark a turnaround point. During a marathon in Belfast (they should have called it Bel*slow*) I was not impressed by the well-meaning encouragement of a local band that had struck up the opening bars of 'When The Saints Go Marching In' as I was approaching. The inconsiderate trumpeters and percussionists were blocking the diagonal shortcut to the next corner. I'm not a fan of jazz anyway and I wasn't going to let these self-important swingers waste my time. I did shout 'sorry', but that was after the bass-drum player had nearly overbalanced backwards onto his posterior and the trombonist had been elbowed forward, causing him to let out a note so shrill that even jazz couldn't cope with it. The saints might *march* in, but I was *running* in and that was far more important!

The trombonist can count himself lucky compared to the youngster in a luminous yellow tabard who was in the wrong place at the wrong time as I was fighting for third place in a local cross-country league fixture. The boy was obviously taking his role seriously as he vigorously waved for us to turn right alongside the changing-rooms building. Parents beware! Do not let your children get into the addictive habit of marshalling. The country is full of running maniacs (like me) who pose a danger to your offspring parallel to that of prostitution, hardcore drugs and Simon Cowell.

Now on this October morning in Priory Park, St Neots, Cambridgeshire (ah the catharsis of confession), I wanted to take the fastest line round that bend and no snotty-nosed fifteen-year-old was going to stop me. Maybe he misinterpreted my slight, cycling-inspired, outward drift on the approach, but there was nothing to misinterpret about the 76kg of adrenaline-charged *me* that knocked him clean off his feet and sent him sprawling into the mud. Did I apologise? Quite the opposite actually, for as I quickly regained my speed I managed to comment on his lack of intelligence and compare him to both male and female genitalia, all in just three words! I never did make it into third place and even had a half-hearted look round for the kid after the race so as to blame him (or was it to make my excuses to him?), but without success. Thinking back, I was lucky not to get disqualified.

You don't need me to tell you to put safety first and that no running race is worth putting life and limb at risk for. It seems that many of you *do* need reminding that crossing a white line won't kill you and that the shortest distance between two points is a straight line. When you line up at the start, go to the side that is nearest the direction of the first bend. If the shortest stretch to the end of where you can see you have to run to involves taking in a bit of pavement or crossing the road, check it's safe and just do it! You won't be the only one and the chances are that you will have had to add a few metres to your final tally by having to overtake people or avoid the odd obstruction. By taking the shortest line you are claiming those metres back. Many movements have relied on civil disobedience to succeed and the movement that is your running is no exception!

Whether you are a sprinter or a shuffler, what you have read so far should help you get to that finish line quicker than if you hadn't read it. If you have a race coming up, stop reading this book now! Stay positive, get your personal victory, and then, *only then*, turn the page for the last chapter!

MILE 20

OVER THE LINE

Catch your breath, move on down the funnel and shake the hand of those just in front and behind. Collect your medal or goody bag and live the moment! This is what it was all for: the elation, the sense of achievement; maybe even the glory and the prize. Revel in the congratulations and be sure to congratulate others. Go for a jog to warm down and compare notes with the other runners, telling each other how hard it was 'out there' and how your time would have been 'at least a minute quicker on a fast course'. Hang around for tea and cake, for you have deserved it, and wait for the results to appear so that you can be sure that your wristwatch was not flattering you. Start calling and texting your friends, broadcast your success far and wide! Once you arrive home, get straight on that computer to see if your time is on the world wide web for the whole wide world to see. Work out your **age-graded percentage** using the 'performance calculators' available on many running sites and see your predicted time for other distances. Have a beer, punch the air and keep that grin. Wear the T-shirt, fill in your training diary and highlight your result. Put it on your Facebook page, ring up that aunt that you haven't spoken to for six months, enter a comment on the race website, email the local paper if you must! This is your latest claim to fame, today you are *somebody*.

Next morning you might be still buzzing. Today you can proclaim your success to all your work colleagues. Someone might even put a cutting from the local paper on the notice board. You might exaggerate your lower-limb stiffness to provoke comments that will lead into you being able to further broadcast your accomplishment. By Tuesday you are tired but the high is still there. Tonight you run with your club-mates who will all have seen your result and be queuing up to pat you on the back.

Then comes Wednesday and suddenly there is a big hole in your life. Nobody left to tell, nobody who wants to listen. The T-shirt is in the wash and your partner has kindly tidied the medal away. You walk into the tea-room at work and nobody, but nobody, looks up. So you go back online and look more closely at your time and start to wonder if you could have gone a little bit quicker. The club webpage has a report on the Tuesday track league. You are old news and you don't like it. You want to feel like you felt on Sunday afternoon again and, almost subconsciously, you are back on the Runner's World events page and looking at the fixtures for next weekend.

A running race is very like a luxury Belgian chocolate or a glass of champagne. One never seems enough and if you sit long enough in front of the open box or bottle, your hand will eventually reach out for another. In the space of time it takes to click your mouse and enter a few numbers, you are suddenly on that road again, drawn in by the need to reproduce that buzz that nothing else can replicate. Maybe it is better, sometimes, 'to travel hopeful than to arrive', and many of us can feel complete in that period of preparation and careful planning. Pouring the bubbly and selecting your favourite praline is nothing, however, without the moment of consumption that follows. So training without racing and racing without giving it everything are empty experiences for the competitive athlete.

This is *you* now. You are the racer, the individual defined by your latest performance, and this is how you judge your fellow human beings. You are only as good as your last race and you believe that this is how others assess you too. Every time you do well it is a blessing *and* a curse because you have raised the bar and you know you will have to train even harder to raise it further.

Are you starting to lose friends? Are you bored by their conversation? Your evenings out are less enjoyable because your mind is on tomorrow's training and everything else seems banal and worthless in comparison. The road has become the place where through your running you feel at one with your true self. Running is becoming your religion.

For years my ambition was to make the British elite **duathlon** team. If I ever made it, I thought, I could retire happy. My satisfaction would be total and I would no longer need to prove myself or chase after new sporting challenges. I made the team (just), but I raced badly and though I have the press-cuttings to prove I was there, it was not my proudest moment and I was not fulfilled. I had had a taste of the world of elite sports performance, yet I was not convinced I belonged there. As Smokey Robinson told us, 'a taste of honey is worse than none at all'. Of course there is *always* another step up because none of us can hope to rule the sporting world, and as athletes we are therefore condemned to permanent dissatisfaction. Some of us can convince ourselves that we are great and can even convince others of the same. The glass may be half-full, our cup maybe even 'spilleth over', but deep down we know that the champagne soon goes flat.

The truth is that nobody, with the possible exception, if you are lucky, of your parents, really cares how good a runner you are. Unless, that is, your achievements can serve as a positive reflection on themselves. Of course the coach rejoices in his coachee's victories and your spouse may like to bask in reflected glory. Your friends are probably secretly hoping they will beat you one day, and your running mates already have the back-stabbing knives sharpened. Notice how encouraging they all used to be as you started out and rose through the ranks towards their level. Suddenly you mutated from plucky underdog into serious threat and the pats on the back became nods of acceptance or wariness. As a runner you may attain your own little celebrity status but your public is fickle and your fame is destined to be short-lived. Admiration turns to expectation and when you fail to meet its demands you will be dismissed and your former admirers will look elsewhere for a new kid on the block.

So we find ourselves asking the same questions as when we first laced up our trainers and took our initial steps into the quirky and peculiar milieu of distance running. What is the point? Is it worth it? With every second per mile that we gain, after every personal best or every marathon that we complete, nothing can convince us that it isn't. The euphoria and the subsequent hubris and swagger with which we find ourselves endowed cannot be matched in other areas of our lives. Running becomes, at least in part, a reason for living. For health reasons some of us 'run to live' but soon we find ourselves living to run. The exercise becomes an addiction, a duty, a responsibility to ourselves that we feel obliged to fulfil. It becomes a cause of stress as well as a solution for it and it starts to put a strain on our relationships. We realise that to attain that same intoxicating feeling of triumph we have to try that much harder and run that much further. We are travelling along a road where, as in life, it is impossible to perform a U-turn.

One day it hits us that we are not enjoying our running as we used to and we dare to let the previously unthinkable enter our minds. Why don't I just give it up? The idea is like a kick in the stomach, and it takes our breath away. It's like being dumped by text with no previous warning. A week without running throws our life off-balance, it's like the earth coming off its axis.

The alarm rings at six and I realise that I don't *have* to get up for a run. My body can't go back to sleep and I make a cup of tea and sit and ponder. I hear the patter of a passing runner go by the front door and I can picture him. It's the old guy with the Boston Marathon T-shirt that I wave to every morning. Maybe he is wondering where I am, asking himself if I am injured or if I have gone away for a training camp. I go to the bathroom and in the mirror I see a guilty expression on a face that wants to be outside. I see cheekbones that only my running has made it possible to decipher. I see deep-set eyes with a cold stare that sees the finish line at a thousand paces but cannot see the happiness in my home. I see short hair, go-faster hair, and dry lips, anticipating a challenge. I look down at a trim and muscular body that does not betray its years and, behind me, a washing basket piled high with garments soaked in the sweat that bears testimony to the last few days' effort.

Eating breakfast, it feels like I don't deserve it and at lunch a sandwich for once seems more than just a light snack. I find myself jumping three steps at a time where yesterday it was just two and have an urge to keep going up the stairs to the floor above my room. Then I receive a phone call from my regular running buddy who explodes into laughter when I notify him of my decision not to run. Five o'clock till six seems to take an age and I have a cold beer, telling myself that *this* is living, *this* is the fun I was denying myself through my daily miles on the road. Chips and curry sauce and then down to the local pub. Why is it that tonight they are asking me about my running when so many times I have been itching to regale them with stories of my athletic prowess and the conversation has just ping-ponged between football and the weather?

The next morning I feel rough and I don't want to lift my eyes to the mirror. Is this the liberty and relaxation bestowed by not having to run? It obviously is for many and they are just as happy if not happier than I am. I open the door to bring in the milk and out there the autumn sun is shining through the trees and the air is fresh. The lightweight trainers point enticingly to the road, laces undone and spread to the sides. Boston Marathon-man toddles by and waves, 'I missed you yesterday!' he laughs.

Running is absurd, but so is *not* running and so is life. Like a monk entering a monastery, becoming a runner is a life-changing event, or at least it can be. You can keep it as just a hobby but then you are not a runner, you are someone who happens to run. Running is me, but so are a hundred other things, and I can keep it in perspective despite the hold it has over me.

Racing gives my running meaning and motivates my training. It doesn't pay the rent and, aside from the debatable health benefits, it serves no useful purpose. I laugh at the importance I give to it, knowing that it is all a self-imposed psychological ploy to improve my performance on that day.

So what about you? Are you prepared to give yourself to endurance sport, to give yourself to running? Do you have the desire to keep pushing through the twenty-mile wall, to break through the Vaseline barrier and to make your nipples bleed? If you do I'll see you out there: in front of me or miles behind, it makes no odds. If you see me laughing, I'm only laughing at myself. I have remembered to add a pinch of salt, have you?

WARM DOWN

The ethos, the modus operandi of this 'Facebook generation' seems to be to try and suck the juice out of every moment for half your life and then spend the rest of it telling the world all about it. Runners are not exempt from this as they detail every session in their profile entries. Maybe through writing this book I have committed the same offence but that was certainly not my intention.

I wanted to make you snigger and to recognise some home truths. I wanted to show that running is not just physiology and science, supplements and training schedules, but also art and philosophy. 'Philosophy' means love of wisdom and through running we stretch our limits and learn more about ourselves and our relationship with the world than we ever could through a computer-simulated model or a television programme.

When a baby goes to the mother's breast it will suck the life-giving milk for all it is worth. Sometimes the vigour can be too much. The nipple may crack and bleed, illustrating that wanting the most from life can cause trauma and pain. So it is with running. To suck the most out of your running you have to be ready to see and taste blood.

'Bleeding Nipples' has one final use. It is for when you are in the middle of your race and you are starting to question your chances of achieving the result you are striving for. As you drive through the pain, repeat the phrase to dictate the rhythm and the intensity of your running. Each syllable marks the contact point of foot on road. 'One, two, three, four! Bleeding Nipples, Bleeding Nipples, Bleeding Nipples, Bleed….' The beat and significance of those words will *refuse* to let you slow down.

GLOSSARY

10k Ten kilometres. An extremely popular racing distance equal to 6.2137 miles.

ACHILLES Legendary Greek warrior who was dipped into the River Styx by his mother Thetis to make him invulnerable. His heel was the only part of his body that was not covered and Achilles was eventually killed by an arrow wound to the heel. The Achilles tendon attaches the calf and soleus muscles to the heel bone.

AEROBIC Exercise in which the muscles draw on oxygen in the blood and therefore has to be of moderate intensity only.

AGE-GRADED PERCENTAGE Various methods exist for relating your performance to your age. Many websites have calculation facilities where you enter your age and the time and distance for your race and you are given a percentage which basically relates your time to the world best by somebody of your age. These percentages are used principally by older athletes and are often referred to as WAVA (World Association of Veteran Athletes) gradings.

ANAEROBIC THRESHOLD The level of intensity of exercise at which lactate is produced at a faster rate than that at which it can be removed or metabolised.

ANSWERS! 800m at three-hour marathon pace should take 204 seconds (3 minutes 24 seconds).

BAUHAUS Punky/goth/glam group at their height in the early eighties.

BLOCKHEAD Ian Dury and the Blockheads, a group famous for the song 'Sex & Drugs & Rock & Roll'.

BODY CIRCUITS A series of exercises which can be adapted to requirements but which usually contain the likes of sit-ups and press-ups. Body circuits are an excellent way to get fit and they hurt!

BPM Beats Per Minute.

BURPEES Squat thrusts with the addition of a jump or just a return to vertical standing position after the knees come forward between the elbows. They work the quadriceps and, yes, they hurt.

BONK Fatigue resulting from glycogen depletion, very common in cycling and often quite sudden and drastic.

CADENCE The rate or frequency with which your legs move in cycling or running. Your running speed depends on a combination of your cadence and your stride length.

CANICROSS Cross-country running with dogs!

CARBS (CARBOHYDRATES) An ideal source of energy for the body, a carbohydrate is an organic compound of carbon, hydrogen and oxygen in a 1:2:1 ratio.

CARBO-LOADING Bringing glycogen levels to a maximum in the lead-up to an endurance effort by eating lots of carbohydrate-rich food. Its efficacy has been questioned.

CARDIOVASCULAR SYSTEM The heart, the lungs, the blood vessels and the blood.

CORE CONDITIONING What the core consists of exactly is up for debate, but core conditioning seeks to strengthen the midsection of the body, in particular the abdominal and lower back muscles.

CROSS TRAINING Training for one sport by doing another.

CREATINE A naturally occurring organic acid that helps supply energy to muscles. Taken in various forms as a supplement to boost sporting performance.

DEAD HEAT When two (or more) runners cross the finish line together and cannot be separated for the purpose of being awarded finish positions.

DIRECTEUR SPORTIF The French name given to the manager of a professional cycling team. The directeur sportif can usually be seen in the team car, following the race and passing instructions to the riders via the radio system.

DISHING A term also used for horses which in reference to the human running action describes an exaggerated lateral movement of the foot when off the ground.

DORSAL RAISE The opposite of a sit-up: lying on your front and lifting your head and shoulders.

DUATHLON A sport related to triathlon which consists of a run followed by a cycle and then another run. Distances vary but the standard championship format is 10k run, 40k bike, 5k run.

ERGO(METER) Strictly speaking this is any type of machine that measures the work done, but is usually used to refer to indoor rowing machines. The use of these machines has become a sport in itself with various leagues and 'indoor rowing' championships.

FARTLEK The Swedish word for 'speed-play', used to refer to a running session involving different speeds which is less structured than an interval session.

FLASH-MOB A sudden grouping of people in a pre-determined place.

FUN RUNNER The ultimate insult, along with 'jogger', for the serious athlete. The existence of people who actually run for fun has yet to be confirmed.

GARMIN The market leader in GPS navigation devices, worn on the wrist, and used by runners to monitor speed, distance covered and other, less useful, information.

GLYCAEMIC INDEX (G.I.) Scale to measure the effect of foods and drinks on blood sugar levels. A high glycaemic index refers to a fast release of glucose into the bloodstream.

GORETEX This should be GORE-TEX and is the brand name of a breathable material that is virtually guaranteed to keep you dry in any conditions.

HILL REPS Running up (and possibly down) a hill more than once. An excellent training session for improving leg strength, technique and pain tolerance!

HRM Heart Rate Monitor. Usually made up of a chest strap and a wrist-watch for display of the number of beats per minute. Most can have upper and lower limits set so that the monitor will bleep at you annoyingly if you come out of your prescribed heart rate training zone.

HYDRATE Get water inside you!

IAAF The International Association of Athletics Federations. The world-wide governing body of athletics.

INTERVAL SESSION/INTERVAL TRAINING Running repeats of one or more fixed distances or times at a faster pace than your normal steady running. The recovery period between efforts and the intensity and duration of the repeats can be varied as required. Interval sessions are a tried and tested method for improving running speed.

HAWAII IRONMAN Widely regarded as the World Championship of Ironman distance triathlon, although there are rival events, this yearly race in Hawaii involves a 2.4-mile swim, 112-mile cycle section and a full marathon run.

HYPOTHERMIA More than just getting a bit cold, hypothermia occurs when the body's core temperature falls below the 35 degree C mark and we cease being able to function properly.

IRONMAN DISTANCE In kilometres this is a 3.8k swim followed by a 180k bike then a 42k run.

ISOTONIC This refers to a solution that has the same concentration of salt as the normal cells of the body and of the blood. It is also a word used to describe a type of muscle contraction.

KNEE-LIFT The degree to which a runner raises the upper leg, and therefore the knee, during the running motion.

L-CARNITINE Very similar to the amino acid known simply as carnitine, this supplement is used to help with the metabolising of food into energy.

LONG REPS A relative term but generally used to describe repeats of fast running that are well over 400m long or last at least two minutes.

MACROCYCLE A long-term training plan, often covering a period of months, a season or even a four-year period, leading to a particular goal such as the Olympic Games.

MESOCYCLE This is a shorter unit of time which comprises a particular type of training or phase of the macrocycle. Typically a mesocycle for runners will last two to eight weeks.

MULTI-TERRAIN RACE An increasingly popular type of event which involves running on and off road.

THE MUNGIES Most people call it 'the munchies'. Hunger pangs that are known to follow various activities including intercourse, alcohol intake and the smoking of marijuana.

NEGATIVE SPLIT The practice of completing a race or time-trial by running the second half faster than the first.

NON-RUNNER A horse that does not start a race or a human who for some strange reason does not run or understand the mentality of those of us that do.

ORTHOTICS Insoles used in an attempt to correct imbalances or to relieve foot pain.

OXYGEN DEBT When the lungs cannot supply the oxygen that the muscles need. It hurts.

PALMARÈS The record of an athlete's major achievements, this term is in common use in the world of cycling.

PARKRUN 5K A relatively new and growing series of year-round 5k races, free to enter and run on parkland or similar in various locations around the country.

PB Personal Best; the best time you have ever achieved for a particular distance.

POSE RUNNING The name given to a methodology for running, associated with shorter stride lengths, developed by the Russian scientist Nicholas Romanov and used by many elite athletes since the 1980s.

PRONATION The common practice of striking the ground with the outside of the heel and rolling the foot inwards.

QUADS/QUADRICEPS The group of four large muscles situated on the front of the thigh.

QUINOA A protein-rich grain from South America which can provide a welcome alternative to rice.

RACE-BAG CHECKLIST A list of all the bits of kit and associated items that you will need to take with you to a particular event. Preparing a list in advance avoids last-minute panic and the chance of forgetting something important.

RACING FLATS Lightweight running shoes with very little cushioning made specifically for racing on the road.

REP A 'repeat' or 'repetition', which refers to the distance or time for the periods of fast running in an interval session.

RECOVERY PERIOD In an interval session this refers to the period between the fast efforts, which may be spent jogging, walking or even still. The term can also be used for the off-season, or part of the year when the athlete backs off from hard training or competition.

RUNNING EQUIVALENT A term used to refer to the way in which we can equate the time spent doing other physical activity to a comparable amount of running. This is often done in terms of perceived effort or calorie consumption.

SEB COE/STEVE OVETT ERA The period including the Moscow (1980) and Los Angeles (1984) Olympic Games when the pair dominated middle-distance running, winning medals and breaking world records.

SITTING ON THE WHEEL A disparaging term which refers to sitting in the slip-stream of another cyclist, which reduces the amount of effort required at a certain speed when compared to cycling alone.

SHORT REPS A relative term but generally used to describe repeats of fast running that are up to 400m long or last less than two minutes.

SPEEDWORK Any running session that involves periods of running at faster than race pace.

SPIKES Studded racing shoes. Specific types are available for the track and for cross-country running.

SPIN To pedal rapidly in an easy gear, which usually means 85 revolutions per minute or over.

SPINNING Exercising on a purpose-built indoor cycle. Spinning classes are often to music and involve a lot of fast pedalling. Bring a towel for the sweat!

SPLIT/SPLITS/SPLIT TIMES The time taken to complete each repeat during an interval session or the various sections of a race or time-trial.

STROKE VOLUME The amount of blood that the heart can pump out with one beat. Consistent prolonged aerobic exercise can improve stroke volume and as a consequence reduce resting heart rate.

SUPINATION The less common opposite of pronation, supination occurs when the runner lands on the inside of the heel and rolls the foot outwards.

TAPER Reducing training load in the lead-up to a race to ensure there is no residual tiredness on the day of competition and to allow the benefits of previous training to take effect.

TRANSITION In triathlon, the part of the race between the swim and cycle sections and between the cycle and run phases. The clock is still ticking during this time.

TREADMILL Basically an electronically powered rolling carpet for running on without moving forward. Better versions allow for decent speeds to be reached and for adjustment of the incline to simulate running uphill. Speeds displayed often flatter!

WALL-SITS An exercise for the quadriceps and core muscles which involves sitting against the wall with thighs parallel to the ground and feet flat on the floor. Extra pain can be added by holding a weight at the same time.

WAFFLE Not a sweet but a shoe with moulded studs ideal for fell running.

WATER RUNNING Replicating the running motion in water. Used as a type of cross training and for rehabilitation after injury.

X-TRAINING Nothing rude, just another way of writing cross training (see above).

Printed in Great Britain
by Amazon.co.uk, Ltd.,
Marston Gate.